Father Comes Home From the Wars

Parts 1, 2 & 3

Suzan-Lori Parks

A SAMUEL FRENCH ACTING EDITION

SAMUEL FRENCH

FOUNDED 1830

SAMUELFRENCH.COM
SAMUELFRENCH-LONDON.CO.UK

FOR PRODUCTION ENQUIRIES

UNITED STATES AND CANADA
Info@SamuelFrench.com
1-866-598-8449

UNITED KINGDOM AND EUROPE
Plays@SamuelFrench-London.co.uk
020-7255-4302

Each title is subject to availability from Samuel French, depending
upon country of performance. Please be aware that *FATHER COMES
HOME FROM THE WARS, PARTS 1, 2 & 3* may not be licensed by
Samuel French in your territory. Professional and amateur producers
should contact the nearest Samuel French office or licensing partner to
verify availability.

IMPORTANT BILLING AND CREDIT REQUIREMENTS

If you have obtained performance rights to this title, please refer to your licensing agreement for important billing and credit requirements.

FATHER COMES HOME FROM THE WARS, PARTS 1, 2 & 3 was first produced at The Public Theater (Oskar Eustis, Artistic Director; Patrick Willingham, Executive Director) in New York City on October 28, 2014. The performance was directed by Jo Bonney, with sets by Neil Patel, costumes by ESosa, lighting by Lap Chi Chu, and sound by Dan Moses Schreier. Songs and additional music were by Suzan-Lori Parks, with arrangements by Steven Bargonetti. The Production Stage Manager was Evangeline Rose Whitlock. The cast was as follows:

THE MUSICIAN . . . . Steven Bargonetti

Part 1: A Measure of a Man

The Chorus of Less Than Desirable Slaves:

    LEADER . . . . Russell G. Jones

    SECOND . . . . Julian Rozzell Jr.

    THIRD . . . . Tonye Patano

    FOURTH . . . . Jacob Ming-Trent

THE OLDEST OLD MAN . . . . Peter Jay Fernandez

HERO . . . . Sterling K. Brown

PENNY . . . . Jenny Jules

HOMER . . . . Jeremie Harris

Part 2: A Battle in the Wilderness

A COLONEL, IN THE REBEL ARMY . . . . Ken Marks

SMITH, A CAPTIVE UNION SOLDIER . . . . Louis Cancelmi

HERO, THE COLONEL'S SLAVE . . . . Sterling K. Brown

Part 3: The Union of My Confederate Parts

THE RUNAWAY SLAVES . . . . Russell G. Jones, Tonye Patano
                                                 and Julian Rozzell Jr.

HOMER . . . . Jeremie Harris

PENNY . . . . Jenny Jules

ODYSSEY DOG . . . . Jacob Ming-Trent

ULYSSES . . . . Sterling K. Brown

FATHER COMES HOME FROM THE WARS, PARTS 1, 2 & 3 then opened at the American Repertory Theater (Diane Paulus, Artistic Director) in Cambridge, Massachusetts, on January 28, 2015. The design and production personnel remained the same. The cast was:

THE MUSICIAN..............................Steven Bargonetti

Part 1: A Measure of a Man

The Chorus of Less Than Desirable Slaves:

     LEADER ....Charlie Hudson III

     SECOND.................................Julian Rozzell Jr.

     THIRD .... Tonye Patano

     FOURTH...................Jacob Ming-Trent/Patrena Murray

THE OLDEST OLD MAN.......................... Harold Surratt

HERO ....Benton Greene

PENNY..Jenny Jules

HOMER...................................... Sekou Laidlow

Part 2: A Battle in the Wilderness

A COLONEL, IN THE REBEL ARMY.....................Ken Marks

SMITH, A CAPTIVE UNION SOLDIER................ Michael Crane

HERO, THE COLONEL'S SLAVE ....Benton Greene

Part 3: The Union of My Confederate Parts

THE RUNAWAY SLAVES ....Charlie Hudson III, Tonye Patano,

                                           and Julian Rozzell Jr.

HOMER...................................... Sekou Laidlow

PENNY..Jenny Jules

ODYSSEY DOG ....Jacob Ming-Trent/Patrena Murray

ULYSSES ....Benton Greene

FROM THE AUTHOR'S *ELEMENTS OF STYLE*

I'm continuing the use of my slightly unconventional theatrical elements. Here's a road map.

(Rest)

Take a little time, a pause, a breather; make a transition.

A Spell

An elongated and heightened *(Rest)*. Denoted by repetition of figures' names with no dialogue. Has sort of an architectural look:

    HERO.
    HOMER.
    HERO.
    HOMER.

This is a place where the figures experience their pure true simple state. While no action or stage business is necessary, directors should fill this moment as they best see fit.

PRODUCTION NOTES

Staging: Sometimes indicated by "*(Aside)*" but most often not, throughout these plays, I'm widely employing the convention of direct address. Enjoy.

Music: I've written songs for these plays. We had a musician on stage, visible and "witnessing" and "interacting" with the characters and audience. Most often the musician will sing the songs. In Part 2 (but not in Parts 1 and 3) the characters sing. Lyrics are in the text. Music's in the back of the book. Also, I've written several musical themes which we used as underscoring or punctuation throughout the show. The musical themes are to supplement the dialogue and stage action. Place the songs where indicated. Future publication may provide indication of the musical themes' specific placement, but, in the meantime, place them judiciously in relationship to their corresponding character or situation.

Returning is the Way of the Tao.
—*Tao Te Ching*, **Verse XL**

Part 1

A Measure of a Man

(The **MUSICIAN** *sings:)*

DARK IS THE NIGHT

DARK IS THE NIGHT
LONG IS THE DAY
DARK IS THE NIGHT
LONG IS THE DAY
GOT TIME FOR WORK
NO TIME TO PRAY.

HE'S HEADING OUT
OR WILL HE STAY.

THE SUN HE HIDES
DON'T SEE HIS FACE
THE NIGHT HE CROWDS
AND DEATH DON'T LEAVE A TRACE.
DARK IS THE NIGHT
BUT THERE'S NO RESTING PLACE.

*(Early Spring, 1862. A slave cabin in the middle
of nowhere.)*

(Far West Texas. One hour before dawn.)

(The **CHORUS LEADER** *measures the night by
holding a hand up to the sky.)*

(After a moment, the **LEADER** *is joined by the*
SECOND.)

LEADER.

LEADER.

LEADER.

SECOND.

How much time we got?

LEADER.

How much you want?

SECOND.

Don't be smart.

Hero's gonna be leaving when the sun comes up.

And we gotta know how long we got till he goes.

LEADER.

Listen to him. Talking like he know.

But we don't know if Hero is going or not.

All we know is the sun's gonna rise, God willing,

But when it comes to Hero,

We gotta wait for his word to know what he's doing.

SECOND.

Me, I'm betting that he's going.

LEADER.

Are you now?

SECOND.

That's right.

LEADER.

You're betting that Hero's gonna go to the War?

SECOND.

That's how I'm betting,

Mark it.

LEADER.

You betting that Hero's going to the War with the Boss-Master?

Working as the Boss-Master's servant-slave?

SECOND.

That's what Hero does here, so that's what he'll do when he goes to the War.

His job ain't gonna change just cause he gets to wear a fancy uniform.

LEADER.

You're betting Hero is gonna wait on Boss-Master hand and foot?

SECOND.

He waits hand and foot on him now.

LEADER.

And hold his horse steady for him to climb on top?

And hold his horse again for him to climb on down?

And run behind, carrying all Boss-Master's whatnots on his back?

Running behind the Boss-Master and the Boss-Master's horse both?

And getting spattered with flecks of dirt

From Boss-Master's horse's hooves?

And getting speckled with bits of bad-smelling release

From that same horse's privates?

And combing down the horse after a long day of fighting?

Scrubbing the horse? Then scrubbing the Boss-Master?

Then putting the Master to bed?

Then combing the Master's coat

And shining his boots.

And Boss-Master, the Colonel, sleeping inside

On a warm cot inside a warm tent.

And Hero, the slave, sleeping outside on the cold hard ground

While the cannons pound and the bullets fly

And the war-wounded holler

Cause their legs and arms are lost, and their hopes are dashed.

SECOND.

Why you got to go on and on about it?

LEADER.

I'm just making sure you know what you're talking about.

SECOND.

I'm betting Hero's going to the War.

LEADER.

With the Boss-Master?

SECOND.

Yep.

LEADER.

As the Boss-Master's slave?

SECOND.

That is what I'm betting. Mark it.

LEADER.

You got time to change your mind.

SECOND.

I'm not changing my mind.

I'm all decided on it.

I just want to know how long we got until sunrise

Cause that's when I'm gonna collect my share of the winnings.

Sounds like you're betting the other way.

LEADER.

I am.

SECOND.

You betting that Hero will give up his chance

At greatness to stay here and grub in the dirt?

You betting that, instead of picking a field of battle,

Hero is gonna pick a field of cotton and corn?

That Hero's gonna want a rusty plow for planting

Instead of a shiny medal for bravery?

That he's gonna choose coveralls instead of a uniform?

That he'll be satisfied with having his name only wrote down

In the Boss-Master's counting-book

Instead of getting a chance at getting his name, Hero,

Maybe wrote up in one of them great Histories?

Now you betting Hero's gonna stay home, so you betting for all that?

LEADER.

Mark it.

And I got a good chance at winning too.

As good a chance as him, anyhow. And we'll see soon enough.

We got about an hour before the sun comes up.

SECOND.

Don't look like an hour to me.

LEADER.

Measure it yourself then.

(**SECOND** *holds a hand to the sky, measuring the night as best he can.*)

LEADER.

What you betting?

SECOND.

My spoon.

LEADER.

I thought you was gonna be buried with that spoon.

SECOND.

I'm betting it but I'm gonna win it back right away

Cause Hero is going to the War.

Mark it!

LEADER.

I'm betting my shoes.

SECOND.

Both of them?

Oh, winter is gonna be cold for you.

You gonna be shoeless and your feet gonna

Freeze and turn blacker than they are now

And then Missus is gonna chop them off

Cause they'll be frozen. Cause they'll be frost-bit-dead.

And you gonna be walking around like Homer do

But worse:

Homer used to have two feet and now he don't got but
   one feet.

But Hero, on the other hand, Hero is as he was born:

Big, brave, smart, honest and strong.

The favorite.

He ain't missing nothing.

LEADER.

Except maybe the War. Snap.

SECOND.

Please.

Anyone else bet?

LEADER.

Not yet.

SECOND.

Not Penny? Not the Old Man?

LEADER.

Nobody yet but you and me.

SECOND.

Them two got more sway on Hero than all of us put
together.

LEADER.

If Hero goes he'll be missing them: Penny and the Old
Man both.

SECOND.

Here are the others

Let's see what they say.

> *(The other* **CHORUS** *members enter, ready to place
> their bets and trying their hands at measuring the
> night.)*

THIRD.

How much time we got?

LEADER.

A little less than an hour now.

SECOND.

Some of us are betting that Hero's going to the War.

LEADER.

And some of us are betting that he'll stay.

FOURTH.

You might be the best at measuring Night

But that don't mean you the best at measuring Men.

THIRD.

Early risers have their say but we gotta make our own
choices on this

Each of us gotta make a measure of the man

We gotta choose for ourselves.

(Rest)

I got a brass button

I might be betting that Hero is—

Going to the War.

FOURTH.

I got a banjo.

THIRD.

Don't bet that.

FOURTH.

I'm betting it. And maybe I'll bet—

That Hero stays put.

LEADER.

There is a kind of sport to be had

In the consideration of someone else's fate.

THIRD.

Where's Penny?

SECOND.

Still in her house most likely.

THIRD.

And the Oldest Old Man?

LEADER.

He woke up early this morning

And he went out in the field to die of shame cause his
    son won't be going.

SECOND.

Or he's dead of fear cause his son will be going.

FOURTH.

Either way sounds like the Old Man is most likely dead.

THIRD.

It happens. He was pretty much as old as a person
    should get.

LEADER.

Woah.

(The **OLD MAN** *enters.)*

CHORUS.

OLD MAN.

CHORUS.

OLD MAN.

OLD MAN.

Why you all crouching away from me?

It's just the Old Man here.

LEADER.

Old Man, you dead yet?

OLD MAN.

What kind of foolish question is that?

Good thing you all ain't free.

Good thing they days ain't they own to fill.

Good thing they time is still owned by the Boss-Master,

Cause, if they time ever was they own, mark it:

They'd be filling it all up with foolishness.

Seeing me standing here but thinking me dead.

Goodness, people, I was just out walking, out looking
  for Hero's dog.

FOURTH.

Hero's dog, the dog called Odd-See.

We all know where Odd-See Dog is at:

Hero's dog is by Hero's side, just like he always is.

OLD MAN.

The dog's run off,

Where he's gone to I don't know.

THIRD.

That's hard to believe.

Hero's dog,

The dog with eyes that go this way and that?

OLD MAN.

Hero's only got one dog.

SECOND.

There must have been something he was chasing.

OLD MAN.

He weren't chasing nothing

Hero kicked that dog.

And then the dog run off.

THIRD.

Old Man, you know Hero don't kick his dog.

OLD MAN.

And Odd-See, his dog, he don't run off neither.

But I'm telling you: both them things happened, mark it.

LEADER.

Strange news. How will it sway your bets?

FOURTH.

Strange news on any day but especially today.

Cause of the bond Hero and Odd-See got between them.

THIRD.

The Dog is always by Hero's side.

SECOND.

The Dog lives in Hero's footsteps.

FOURTH.

All his food comes from Hero's plate.

LEADER.

And the shade he takes comes from Hero's shadow.

OLD MAN.

And the dog is Hero's good luck charm.

Don't forget about that.

LEADER.

Now that's just some superstitious nonsense!

OLD MAN.

I'm telling you what I know for true.

Listen up:

Penny, she comes out the door

And when Hero said the dog had run off she got worrisome.

Then, Hero and Homer together, they headed on up to the house.

And Penny, left alone, she fell on her knees and prayed a quiet prayer:

For Odd-See to come back.
She finished praying on her knees
Then she went praying on her feet.
She walked off, went looking for the dog.
I followed her but I followed slow.
Got tired, headed back, here I am.

LEADER.

How are you betting, Old Man?

SECOND.

Will Hero stay or head to the War?

OLD MAN.

I ain't ready to reveal my say.

LEADER.

Still thinking about that dog.

OLD MAN.

It's a consideration.
That dog is Hero's luck.
It's as simple as that.

THIRD.

The sun's coming soon.
And Hero will get himself decided.
Dog or no dog.

SECOND.

Don't make a mountain out of a molehill,

FOURTH.

Don't make a god out of a dog, Old Man.

LEADER.

Don't make a snake out of a rope.

OLD MAN.

What I'm telling you is true.
And The Truth will set you free
Even if the Master don't.

CHORUS.

OLD MAN.

CHORUS.

OLD MAN.

OLD MAN.

That's Hero coming now.

> (**HERO** *enters, coming back from the big House.*)
>
> (*He carries a pair of boots and some worn-out pieces of a Confederate Army uniform. The day's events and their possibilities have created an air of excitement within him. A buoyancy.*)

HERO.

Morning.

ALL.

Morning Hero.

HERO.

You all all awake, huh?

LEADER.

We're waiting on you, Hero.

HERO.

Where's my dog?

Why don't he come to greet me?

OLD MAN.

Penny's gone to bring him back.

He's probably out there curled up in a warm spot, sleeping.

LEADER.

It's still early yet.

SECOND.

Everything with any sense is still asleep.

HERO.

Count us among the senseless then. And Boss-Master-Boss the most senseless of us all. He's been up awake the whole night working on getting ready and he's still busy at it. I was trying to decide my mind while I was helping him. And he knew it too. He kept giving me these looks. But under his watch ain't no place for this man to think. So I had to excuse myself and come back here with my mind as unmade as my bed!

(Rest)

Boss had me and Homer both helping him get dressed. Homer, after all his years of working outside minding the mules, he ain't much of a valet, but it turned out all right. All them uniform whatnots. Boss gave me these remnants to wear, if I choose to go.

OLD MAN.

Boss' uniform must be a fine thing.

HERO.

You'll see it soon enough. All the sashes and belts and buckles and braids. If I hadn't of known, I'd think Boss-Master-Boss was decorating himself to join the traveling circus. He's got this hat with a cream-colored feather that's as big as a fan, hell, it's bigger than a fan, that feather is twice the size of Boss-Master's head. I hope the wind don't blow on it else it'll blow him right off his horse. And his new boots. To get them on he had to tug and stomp and cuss so much, Missus comes in running thinking that me and Homer had attacked Boss-Master. That thought alone is funny. Ha, you shoulda seen it. Boss-Master, sitting on the bed with Missus fanning him cause his boots, they fit, but they so new-tight, you know. And then Homer said, "Lucky you don't got to walk to the War." And that's when Boss-Master laughed.

(Rest)

You all gonna head up to the House to see him head out?

OLD MAN.

He's promised each of us a coin for our trouble so we'll be there, mark it.

HERO.

Maybe you'll be waving goodbye to me too. But maybe not.

(Rest)

Go get some rest, now. Unless night turning into day is suddenly something special to see.

LEADER.

Are you going or are you going to stay?

SECOND.

Some of us will bet you'll go.

FOURTH.

Others'll bet the other way.

THIRD.

What will you decide, Hero?

OLD MAN.

Listen to you all

Feeding on Hero's choice

Like so many buzzards feed.

Cept the carcass ain't one. He's still living.

So let's step away.

HERO.

You all clutching ahold of your best treasures.

Odd-See!

OLD MAN.

Plenty of time for him to come home.

HERO.

I'm starting to think that dog ain't nothing.

A dog is just a dog.

A dime a dozen.

OLD MAN.

Sit. Rest.

Penny's out looking for him

And we'll sit and watch the dawn come up.

Mark it with us.

*(**HERO** sits with them, measuring the night.)*

HERO.

CHORUS.

HERO.

CHORUS.

HERO.

Why don't my dog come back, do you think?

OLD MAN.

Don't think on it.

Just sit.

HERO.

I need peace or quiet at least.

You all go help look for my dog, huh?

FOURTH.

We jump when you say jump.

THIRD.

We follow you, even if it's just your finger, pointing out
the way.

*(They go. The **OLD MAN** slowly follows them.)*

HERO.

Father.

Stay with me awhile.

OLD MAN.

"Father."

I love it when you call me that.

HERO.

If you could have anything you wanted

Could you name it?

OLD MAN.

You granting wishes?

HERO.

Would you have your son go to the War or would you
have him stay?

OLD MAN.

I bet you already know your father's mind.

HERO.

Not until I hear it from his mouth.

When I say "War" I try to read your face

But you sense me looking and you turn away.

OLD MAN.

I want you to decide your own self.

Boss-Master ordering you to go to the War with him

And then he tells you that you got a choice in the
matter.

The great Boss-Master-Boss gives you your freedom of
choice.

Like he figures his freedom of choice is gonna
somehow

Take the place of the Rightful Freedom that he's been
denying you.

Like he figures that his gift, his little crumb of choice,

Will somehow save his soul when the Judgment Day
comes.

Me and Penny both agreed to stay clear and let the last
word on it be up to you.

HERO.

Still still still: Do you want me staying home?

OLD MAN.

Yes.

HERO.

You want me staying here? Did I hear right?

OLD MAN.

Lemmie shine up your boots for you.

Keep my hands busy.

(The **OLD MAN** *shines* **HERO**'*s boots.)*

OLD MAN.

> What father in his right mind wants his son going off
>   to the War?
>
> I mean, yes, well, maybe real fathers.
>
> Lucky men who had their sons shot out into life
>   through their own balls
>
> Maybe they figure easy come easy go.
>
> You're my son but as you know
>
> I didn't make you from my spit.
>
> Which makes me, I guess, a fake-father.
>
> But you, Hero, no mistake, you're a real son through
>   and through.
>
> No, we don't got the luxury of blood between us,
>
> And your arrival was a happenstance, but all that makes
>   me
>
> Double-bless the day you came here and looked up to
>   me.
>
> And here I am now. Looking up to you.
>
> Oh, I wish I was your real daddy.
>
> Then I could say I knew your Ma.
>
> Cause you got at least half your self from your Ma,
>
> Which means that Woman was a Force Divine.
>
> So if I had known her even for a quick minute: Woah!
>
> I'd still, after all these years, I'd still have that sweet gal
>   on my mind.
>
> Lord! I ain't never even met her,
>
> So stop me, son, from crying cause she's gone.

HERO.

> You can always get me laughing.
>
> Even when things are weighing heavy.

OLD MAN.

> I want you to go, son.
>
> There. I said it. I'll tell you true:
>
> I want you to go to the War.

HERO.

There's Truth in your voice now.

OLD MAN.

Yes.

HERO.

This morning when Boss and me spoke alone together

He promised me:

My Freedom for My Service.

OLD MAN.

Your Freedom?

Your Freedom for your Service?

All the more reason. You'll go now, surely.

Mark it!

I'm readying myself to wave goodbye.

HERO.

Not just yet.

He dangled it in front of me. My Freedom.

Like a beautiful carrot.

Like a diamond. And those scraps of uniform and the diamond Freedom glittered

As he promised it, asking me to see it, to smell it, touch it, try it on for size.

But while I so wanted to I was still thinking on the bald fact that in his service

I will be helping out

On the wrong side.

That sticks in my throat and makes it hard to breathe.

The wrong of it.

All those days working in his fields that I thought of killing him.

You know those days. I'd come home in a sweat

Not from working but from the rage.

And Penny, understanding but bearing on, like we all do.

I'd be out in those fields behind a plow praying for his murder.

How can I last one day on the battlefield

Without doing the same or worse?

OLD MAN.

Kill him and there's no life for you.

HERO.

I know.

I won't hurt him. There's my Word.

But can you see Boss-Master and me coming home from the War

And him giving me my Freedom like he says he will?

OLD MAN.

It's right for you to wonder.

After the way he promised you your Freedom that first time.

Why do you shiver?

HERO.

Just the memory of it.

His First Promise. His very First Promise.

OLD MAN.

That was the only other time he offered you your Freedom.

Unless I'm mistaken.

HERO.

Father?

OLD MAN.

Son?

HERO.

Nothing.

OLD MAN.

Boss-Master promising in front of everybody and in a loud voice:

"I'll give you your Freedom if you cut off Homer's foot,"

And you said, "No!" You bravely refused him.

So Boss threatened you with death

And then the axe came down.

Mark it: Yes, it was horrible

But right now: this Promise is—more promising.

He'll come through this time, son.

Your Service for him and for his Cause will outweigh
     everything

And he'll come through.

HERO.

I'll chance it if you feel so sure.

I'll accept his offer. Take him up on his Promise.

And I'll give myself a chance at something great.

And I'll come back here.

And I'll help everybody when I get home.

I'm as good as gone.

OLD MAN.

Put on your uniform.

HERO.

It's not a whole uniform.

More like a bunch of scraps.

OLD MAN.

Put it on and wear it.

A man like you can make a wholesome thing out of bits
     and pieces.

> (**HERO** *puts on the scraps of his Confederate Army
> uniform.*)

HERO.

I can see myself, out there.

Guns blazing all around, cannons going off

And the line of endless tents

And the piles of the dead.

OLD MAN.

You won't be one of the dead, son.

You do your service and then

Here you are coming home.

I can see you.

Walking bravely

HERO.

And I bow down to you, giving thanks, glad to be back.

OLD MAN.

And your Freedom has been granted

And your dog has been found

And none of your limbs have been lost.

HERO.

Mark it.

OLD MAN.

You all dressed?

HERO.

Pretty much.

OLD MAN.

Look at you.

How do you look?

HERO.

I look all right.

OLD MAN.

Parade around.

Lemmie hear your boots marching in the dirt.

> (**HERO** *parades around. He styles and profiles.*)

> (**PENNY** *enters. Her presence stops him in his tracks.*)

HERO.

Hold my hand.

PENNY.

Oooh it's warm.

Look at me, I'm dancing you!

> (*She moves his arms, making him dance.*)

> (*He lifts her up.*)

HERO.

And I'm flying you!

PENNY.

I'm a bird!

(They embrace. It's deep.)

HERO.

Close your eyes.

PENNY.

They're closed.

HERO.

Kiss?

(They kiss.)

HERO.

Keep them closed. Now look.

PENNY.

HERO.

HERO.

I was just trying it out.

PENNY.

There's planting to be done today

You gonna wear them whatnots and them boots walking behind the plow?

HERO.

I was just seeing how it felt.

PENNY.

Feels hot, don't it? If it don't yet it will soon.

HERO.

What do you think?

PENNY.

I think— I think the day's gonna be warm.

And you all dressed up like that and plowing the field—

I think you'll be sweating like the old folks do when
  they see a holy miracle.

And I think it'll take you twice as long to get done half
  as much

And then everybody would know what I know looking
  at you now:

They'd say, "Hero, the man who is practically Penny's
  husband,

That man Hero has gone and lost his mind."

OLD MAN.

He's got something to tell you, girl.

If you'd just give him a clearing.

PENNY.

Tell me what, Hero?

HERO.

We've been discussing things.

PENNY.

I'm ready to add my say.

OLD MAN.

You filled up both my ears already.

HERO.

Head to toe, Penny: How do I look?

PENNY.

That outfit makes you better-looking, Hero, I can't lie.

HERO.

Not every man can wear it well.

HERO.

PENNY.

PENNY.

Let's go inside

And stay in bed all day.

HERO.

And miss the War?

PENNY.

The War is nothing.

You said as much yourself.

HERO.

You gone looking for the dog?

PENNY.

I did.

But I shoulda stayed here and kept an eye on you.

HERO.

Odd-See ain't come back with you.

PENNY.

Even the Old Man can see that.

The way you look would make someone with less conviction

Think they was too late to put the good sense back into your head

That seems to have drained clean out from spending time with the Old Man.

OLD MAN.

He's made his mind up, woman,

Leave him be.

PENNY.

His mind don't matter none to me

Cause I know what his heart says.

You don't want to disappoint the Old Man but go on and tell him.

He can bear it.

HERO.

HERO.

PENNY.

Hero? Go on.

OLD MAN.

> Don't keep pestering him.
>
> It's natural for a man to want to go to War
>
> To seek his fortune
>
> To try his hand at grabbing better than what he's got now.

PENNY.

> It's also natural for God to strike dead someone as old as you.
>
> Just cause God ain't yet called his name don't mean He forgot.
>
> I'ma remind Him:
>
> "Lord, You got an old old man down here who You shoulda taken a long time ago."

HERO.

> Don't curse, Penny.
>
> Not on my account.
>
> She didn't mean it, father, so the curse, it didn't get to Heaven.
>
> Girl, we went and talked it through, father and me.
>
> Hear me out, hear?
>
> I'm going.

PENNY.

> But you don't want to go.
>
> You don't want to.
>
> You told me so.
>
> Hero, just this morning.
>
> We woke together.
>
> At the same time. In the same breath like we often do.
>
> You breathed it out and I breathed it in.
>
> And we woke up.
>
> No work to do that early so it wasn't the plow calling.
>
> No rooster up that early and not no sun, Hero.
>
> Just us two.
>
> Everything else was quiet and sleep.

"I got to tell you my mind before the others meddle
with me and twist me up," you said.

Cause you knew. You knew that that's what they do.

Planting their own seeds into you.

Using you worse than Boss-Master does.

"I'm not going," you said.

"I'll tell the Master so at sunrise," you said.

"Help me keep my secret," you said.

You leaned close to me, my ear to your lips. In the dark
it was.

Whispering into my ear.

Putting your words into my head.

"I'm not going to the War," you said.

And, oh, oh, I was afeared for you.

Crossing Boss-Master is a horrible thing.

That's what went through my head.

But also, it was sweet

Even though it was terrifying it was sweet.

That you was not gonna raise a hand against your own
cause

That you was not gonna help out Master.

That you would stand up.

That you would stay home.

At least that's what I thought I heard.

OLD MAN.

You woke this morning deciding not to go?

HERO.

Hours ago I might of said that.

I might have thought that out loud

And shared it with Penny, sure.

OLD MAN.

You gave her your Word?

PENNY.

You did.

HERO.

> I gave you some words in the dark while half sleeping.
>
> What man don't do that?
>
> But now I'm decided.
>
> I'm going, girl.

PENNY.

> You go to the War and for what?

HERO.

> I got a chance at getting something.

OLD MAN.

> He can't explain it, Penny
>
> There is a thing about his call to service
>
> That he needs to keep private until the time is right.
>
> So let's all just accept the hard truth:
>
> Hero has been called to serve and he's leaving.

PENNY.

> Without his dog.

HERO.

> The dog will be home directly and if he don't come
> what of it?

PENNY.

> That dog's your luck, Hero.

OLD MAN.

> That's just some superstitious nonsense.
>
> It's time for all of us, if we want to grow out of this low
> place,
>
> To leave behind beliefs like that.
>
> Hero has changed his views and, following his lead,
>
> I've changed my views too.
>
> And so should you.
>
> It's very liberating.

PENNY.

> "Liberating"?

OLD MAN.

"Freeing."

Mark it, woman.

PENNY.

Boss, he must be promising you something wonderful.

He's promising you your Freedom

Something "Liberating,"

Ain't I right?

(Rest)

I'm right. Mark it. That's what's got your head turned.

At first I thought it was the Old Man's words

But, no, Boss, to sell you on it,

He's promising you your Freedom again, ain't he?

Such a sweet promise!

But how could you even think of saying yes to him

When you know good and well

That his Freedom-promise is only. Ever. Linked.

To something. Bad.

HERO.

Quiet!

Quiet please.

HERO.

PENNY.

PENNY.

Hero?

HERO.

Penny?

(Rest)

Daylight will be here shortly.

And here comes everybody.

Coming on back

And they're coming back without my dog.

> *(The* **CHORUS** *enters. The Dog is not with them.)*

HERO.

> Tell me the news.
>
> Tell me how you found him dead.
>
> Tell me quick.
>
> The creature that brought me nothing but luck
>
> Like other dogs bring their masters bones
>
> You found him dead and his body ripped in pieces.
>
> So horrible you didn't have the heart to bring him back in scraps.
>
> Am I right?

LEADER.

> We didn't find nothing.

SECOND.

> Not even a hair.

FOURTH.

> We did see his tracks
>
> But they faded.

THIRD.

> We called out to him
>
> No answer.

OLD MAN.

> So Hero's dog is gone.

LEADER.

> What do you say to that?

SECOND.

> Weigh it all careful.

THIRD.

> Weigh it in your heart.

HERO.

> There's still time before the sun is up.
>
> But, hell, I'm all decided.

LEADER.

> Give us a chance to place our bets

FOURTH.

Cast our votes

SECOND.

Make our sway

THIRD.

Have our say.

HERO.

Keep your treasures close. Don't risk losing them.

I'm not going.

There's my mind.

I'll stay.

LEADER.

It's the wise choice.

PENNY.

You'll stay?

SECOND.

Hero. Hero.

Think on it.

OLD MAN.

Think on it, son.

PENNY.

You'll stay?

HERO.

I'm staying.

Let the day come.

Let Boss-Master come riding up here wondering where
    I'm at.

Let him see the scraps of uniform piled on the ground.

Let him see me standing here with you all.

Let him hear me say, "I'll stay."

Let him come. I'll be standing here.

And I dare that man to move me.

SECOND.

But there will be beatings for all of us

When Boss hears what he's decided.

FOURTH.

> The dog running off was smart.
>
> But where will we go to hide?

THIRD.

> The whip is a long whip.
>
> Boss' anger will come up

LEADER.

> That's right. He'll beat him hard and
>
> He'll beat us twice as hard.

SECOND.

> For his 10 lashes we'll get 20.

THIRD.

> For his 20 we'll get 40.

FOURTH.

> For his 50 we'll get 100.

HERO.

> I won't go. I can't. My heart's been set against it from
> the start.

CHORUS.

HERO.

CHORUS.

HERO.

> *(Rest)*

OLD MAN.

> So you'll have to harm yourself in some way.
>
> To take the edge off Boss' anger.

LEADER.

> A finger or two cut and bleeding

THIRD.

> He'll be wounded.

SECOND.

> Missing a part of himself, maybe.

PENNY.

We'll all say it was an accident.

OLD MAN.

In the heat of getting ready

And in the darkness

FOURTH.

A knife fell in the wrong place

THIRD.

Didn't Boss hear your screams we'll ask him?

HERO.

He'll be up at the House, wondering where I'm at.

LEADER.

And when he comes riding up to see for himself

SECOND.

He'll see Hero. Not standing in defiance,

FOURTH.

But lying wounded on the ground.

OLD MAN.

It'll be all right.

HERO.

I'll harm myself in some bloody way.

OLD MAN.

You'll ease up the harm Boss wants to do to us.

HERO.

I'll do it.

PENNY.

He'll hurt himself to keep us safe.

HERO.

You'll take my foot.

PENNY.

Your foot?!

HERO.

Do like I say.

You'll take my foot.

That seems fair.

PENNY.

No.

OLD MAN.

We'll do it or get beaten dead for his defiance.

One of you will whet the knife.

And Penny, you'll hold him while I make the cut.

> (**LEADER** *whets the knife.* **HERO** *puts his foot on a rock to be cut off.*)

THIRD.

It's still dark out

There's still time to reconsider

Hero you were born perfect and lived your whole life whole

Is that to end here? Is that to end now

In front of a ruined cabin with an old knife?

HERO.

Harm won't come to no one but me.

FOURTH.

Won't some angel come

And hold back the hand?

Where is the big voice

Telling us that all this is just some kind of test

To see if we were willing to follow the path.

Where is the path? Where is the path?!

The path, it isn't marked.

Won't some spirit come down

Some angel, some light, some mercy?

LEADER.

The sun is coming by my measure, mark it.

But the day is getting darker seems to me.

Homer is coming. Maybe we should wait for him.

He might have an idea for this.

SECOND.

Before we worried about our bets

That we'd lose what we laid down.

We were only thinking about winning something
But now, there's Hero, ready to lose a part of himself
To save us from a greater harm that's surely coming.

OLD MAN.

Hold still, son
I've got a sure hand
And a kind heart.

(As the **OLD MAN** *raises the knife,* **HOMER** *enters.)*

CHORUS.

OLD MAN.

HERO.

PENNY.

CHORUS.

HOMER.

Whatchu all up to?

HERO.

You got eyes.

You can see.

HOMER.

So go ahead and do it if you're gonna do it.

Old Man you feel your mark all right?

OLD MAN.

I do.

HOMER.

You got him held good, Penny?

PENNY.

I do.

HOMER.

You decided that you're staying, Hero?

HERO.

I'm decided.

CHORUS.

We'll swear to it.

HOMER.

Cause that's the only reason you all would be organized like this, mark it.

You're gonna spare us Boss-Master's full wrath and fury.

HERO.

I hope to.

HOMER.

You all don't just stand around looking.

Somebody get something to stanch the blood.

Get some rags, plenty of rags.

Get a bucket.

Cause there's gonna be plenty of blood

Remember how it was with me, Hero?

But with you it's not gonna be like it was with me:

Hero won't be having his blood to spilling on the ground

It's hard for a man to see that

Harder than losing his foot I think

To see his blood spilling out on the ground

To see the earth

Drink it up

Greedily drinking, greedy,

And nothing growing back.

And the foot cut off

And left on a pole to rot

Least that's how Boss-Master did mine.

Remember?

Left it on a pole right over there

Dared any of us to take it down.

Hero took it down

And got whipped.

Penny took it down.

And got whipped.

So it stayed up there and rotted.

Hero,

All that talking you was doing with Boss-Master about how

You going to the War with him and you ain't going after all.

HERO.

Too many signs pointing to stay.

Penny's words, the dog not here, my own heart.

OLD MAN.

And my own heart

Frail as it is

Can't no longer raise this knife

Take it Hero

If you need your foot cut off

Then you do it your own self.

HOMER.

Go on, then.

>   (**HERO** *raises the knife but does not bring it down.*)

HOMER.

Yeah.

I'm not the oldest here,

But, Hero, since we come up together

I've known you longest

And I figure maybe, in some respects I know you best.

HERO.

You do.

HOMER.

His knife ain't coming down cause his mind ain't decided.

HERO.

My mind's made up.

HOMER.

Then let the knife come down.

When has one of us ever had a choice except for you,
Hero?

You'll always be lucky.

Go on

Let it fall.

(**HERO** *cannot maim himself.*)

PENNY.

Give it to me then

I'll do it.

(**PENNY** *tries in vain to take the knife from him.*)

LEADER.

You're right, he's not decided yet.

SECOND.

If you were betting, Homer, how would you bet?

FOURTH.

There's so much riding on it.

THIRD.

And poor as we are

Each of us would surely love to take home the winnings.

HOMER.

I'm not betting either way.

HERO.

I thank you.

Everybody has a stake in what I do but you.

HOMER.

Go to the War

Stay Home.

Those your choices?

LEADER.

Those are his choices.

PENNY.

The knife.

HERO.

Take it.

(**HERO** *gives the knife to* **PENNY.**)

HOMER.

I say don't.

HERO.

Don't?

ALL. *(except* **HERO & PENNY** *)*

Don't?

PENNY.

Don't what.

HOMER.

Don't.

PENNY.

He's got to do one or the other, Homer.

Don't make his mind more tangled up than it is already.

HOMER.

He shouldn't do neither.

OLD MAN.

Who needs your raggedy opinion anyhow?

The sun is coming

And Hero's going

And that's his father's word.

PENNY.

The sun is coming

And Hero's staying

And that's the word of the gal he loves best.

HOMER.

Mark it, people

Anybody who wants to win the bet

Mark it:

See how they each pulling on his coat

Penny, she's got her woman's love and she's pulling
   him to stay

Old Man, he's got his father's love and he's pulling him
   away.

Penny, she's got a knife and if Hero stays that'll hurt
   for sure

Old Man, he's got the War waiting, and that'll hurt
   more than 100 knives.

Go to the War or stay at Home?

HERO.

Stop making a game of it.

HOMER.

Ain't no game, Hero.

Cause you shouldn't be doing neither.

Cause you shouldn't stoop

To do neither

Cause both choices, Hero,

To stay here and work the field

To go there and fight in the field

Both choices are

Nothing more than the same coin

Flipped over and over

Two sides of the same coin

And the coin ain't even in your pocket.

HERO.

I'll give you that.

LEADER.

But what else is there for one like us?

SECOND.

We gotta take what we've been handed.

PENNY.

Fieldwork is honest work.

OLD MAN.

But Boss-Master is promising Hero his Freedom.

LEADER.

His Freedom!

OLD MAN.

His Freedom for his Service.

SECOND.

Promising Freedom?

HOMER.

That man will never free you. Ever.

You're waiting for him to give you Freedom

When you should take it.

Yeah.

I been thinking on it.

Boss-Master will be sitting up there, expecting Hero,
     but Hero, see,

Hero will be long-run-off and gone!

"Hero has misplaced himself," Boss-Master will say.

Hells yeah.

I can tell you how to go.

All that mapping I used to do

I still got it all in my head.

I'll tell it to you, Hero.

Mark it, now's the time.

Start running and you'll be free so quick

The War will still be raging and

Master will be promising Freedom to the next fool

Fool enough to believe it.

And you,

You'll have your Freedom already.

Taken.

Taken for yourself

It'll be completely yours.

LEADER.

This idea is a third way

Something to consider.

OLD MAN.

What do you say, son?

PENNY.

I'm ready to stand with whatever you decide.

HERO.

I ain't never been one to run from nothing.

HOMER.

Your father ran away.

HERO.

And look what it got him

Hanging from a tree.

HOMER.

That won't be you.

HERO.

How you know?

HOMER.

So you won't run away cause you're scared?

HERO.

I'm not scared.

FOURTH.

Hero's father was wild but Hero is mild?

HERO.

I'm not scared.

OLD MAN.

What is it then?

HERO.

He promised me.

He gave me his Word.

I want him to make good on what he promised.

HOMER.

You're a fool.

HERO.

Heavy words deserve heavy hands.

HOMER.

> Don't beat me, Hero.
> It won't look right for you
> The one who cut off my foot
> To beat me down.

HERO.

> You shouldn't have tried to run off.
> I told you so back then
> And you got caught
> But I told you
> If you just worked hard
> Everything would be all right
> Years later, here we all are
> Working hard and things are all right, more or less,
> Aren't they?
> Except you don't got your foot.
> If you hadn't tried to run off you could of still had your
>   foot today.
> And I wouldn't have to bear the burden of
> Being the one who was forced to maim you.

HOMER.

> Back then when I run off
> We were supposed to head out together.
> But then I guess you went and changed your mind.
> Boss-Master and his like finding me,
> Surrounding me, dragging me back here.
> And you cutting off my foot.

PENNY.

> You can't blame Hero for that.

HERO.

> He threatened me with death
> Put a gun to my head
> And that's what got the axe to swing.

SECOND.

>   We were all there.

>   We all saw it.

LEADER.

>   Any one of us would have done the same.

>   There's harm in it but no blame.

OLD MAN.

>   My son was only doing his best

>   Caught as we all are between a rock and a hard place.

HOMER.

>   But still the axe came down, didn't it.

HERO.

>   It did.

PENNY.

>   And you'll leave it at that. Please?

>   We've all heard enough.

HOMER.

>   So after what he made you do to me

>   How can you ever believe Boss-Master

>   When he promises you the moon and stars?

HERO.

>   Cause I ain't like you.

>   I ain't some wild man who will

>   Break away from good common sense and

>   Go running. Go running here go running there

>   Go running who knows wherever.

>   No real map no real nothing and getting no real
>   freedom that way.

>   Grabbing, taking, snatching, begging, borrowing,
>   stealing?

>   My Freedom's gonna be free of that.

>   Cause who would I be when I'm free that way?

>   Something stolen. A Stolen-Freedom?

>   That ain't me.

HOMER.

Seems like

After all the wrong Boss has done

You're no better than a dog.

Or worse than your own dog

Who at least had the sense to run off

When his Master kicked.

You're a dog what gets fed scraps from the table

A dog what gets kicked then stays around.

A dog what follows his Master no questions asked.

You're like that Hero.

HERO.

I should of cut off your other foot.

I should of cut off your head.

PENNY.

Peace.

THIRD.

Be kind. Be kind. Make your words gentle.

Counsel him on whether he should go or stay.

But don't make him feel wrong wanting Freedom his
    way.

LEADER.

The sun is coming and Hero is heading one way or
    another.

SECOND.

We want the bonds between you to be good.

FOURTH.

No matter what's decided.

OLD MAN.

Even though you all are owned by another man

Your words are your bond.

They're part of your record.

Words and deeds both.

HOMER.

HOMER.

HOMER.

Did you all know

That it was Hero who lead them to me.

Did you all know that it was Hero who told where
    Homer had run off to.

I was gone but nobody knew which way I'd went.

OLD MAN.

That's a lie

A lie to make confusion.

FOURTH.

We can't believe it.

LEADER.

Set the story right, Hero.

HERO.

I don't recall the circumstances of that day

With this day here crowding in my head

And all you all crowding around me.

SECOND.

Just tell us how it really went.

THIRD.

We don't need a lie about you hanging in the air.

HOMER.

I'll tell you how it went.

Boss told me so.

He was drinking just now he was drinking trying to get
    his courage together

Cause he's going to the War,

And he starts talking to me as if I'm you.

I dunno, Hero, do we look alike?

Cause he confused me for you.

But you had left to come back here, and it was only me
    alone helping him get ready:

And him drunk and thinking I'm you,

Talking, making it be certain-known that, unlike any
promise made before,

This time, his Promise of Freedom would be a sure
thing.

Not like the time before.

And here, ok, I thought he was gonna talk about the
Freedom for the foot

(And how it didn't work out too good)

But he brought up something else:

A time before that:

The First Promise he called it:

The day he promised you your Freedom

In exchange for you telling him which way I'd run off
to.

And how you went and told him.

How you gave me away.

How you pointed them to me.

And still he didn't free you.

"But it wont be like that this time," he said.

"This time I'll come through," he said.

You gave me away.

He told me so.

Then drunk Boss-Master-Boss realizes

That he's telling Homer instead of Hero.

And he went all quiet.

Not another word.

LEADER.

Freedom in exchange for giving Homer away?

And you said yes.

OLD MAN.

Lies.

Homer is nothing but envy and bile.

SECOND.

Freedom in exchange for breaking the bond of trust.

And you said yes.

OLD MAN.

Lies.

HERO.

Believe it.

It's true.

Boss gave me a hundred reasons why I should tell.

OLD MAN.

Why are you lying on yourself, son?

PENNY.

It's true.

Years ago Hero told me

And I've held it in our confidence.

Like he told me to.

THIRD.

Freedom for giving Homer away.

HERO.

Boss told me—

He talked up close inside my ear and he said—

He said—

And thought, I thought—

I don't know what I thought.

HOMER.

When Boss said jump you jumped, that's all.

You told on me to him.

I told on you to Them.

That makes it even.

OLD MAN.

All we've got is the trust between us.

(Rest)

I can't call you son anymore.

LEADER.

And we can't call you Hero.

PENNY.

That's still his name.

THIRD.

Maybe we won't call him anything at all.

(The sun rises.)

CHORUS.

PENNY.

HERO.

HOMER.

CHORUS.

SECOND.

The sun is up.

HERO.

And my need to leave is clear.

Not run off, Homer,

Although I can see there's a value in it,

But it's not my road.

I'll go trot behind the Master.

The non-Hero that I am.

Odd-See!

FOURTH.

He calls his dog

His dog that brings him luck.

HERO.

Odd-See!

SECOND.

Does the dog hear him?

HERO.

Odd-See dog!

LEADER.

The dog no longer knows his voice.

THIRD.

The dog no longer knows his name.

(The Dog does not return.)

HERO.

> The sun is up
> And Boss-Master waits
> I'll go.

HOMER.

> Boss will give each of us a coin for waving them goodbye
> And a whipping if we don't.

PENNY.

> I'll go and wave goodbye
> Then I'll be here. Right here.
> I'll wait for you.

LEADER.

> Let's all go to see him go.
> A broken man on a dark dark day.

> > **(HERO** *exits followed by* **PENNY, HOMER** *and the* **CHORUS**.*)*

> > *(The* **OLD MAN** *rises to go but then sits.)*

OLD MAN.

> To have a son leave home is no small thing
> But losing a son before he leaves
> That's more than an old man can bear.
> I'll sit and wait for his return.
> He promised he'd come home.
> With luck it won't be long.

(The MUSICIAN *sings:)*

HE'S LEAVING

OH, HE'S LEAVING
HE'S LEAVING YOU ALL
AT THE BREAK OF DAY
HE'S LEAVING
ALL YOU ALL
AT THE BREAK OF DAY
DON'T KNOW YET WHERE HE'S HEADING
BUT HE KNOWS HE CANNOT STAY.

AND THE GAL HE LOVES
SHE'S MAKING PERFUME
PERFUME WHEN SHE WALKS
YEAH, THE GAL HE LOVES SHE'S MAKING
PERFUME WHEN SHE WALKS
I WOULDN'T NEVER CROSS HER
SHE WILL CUT YOU LIKE A HAWK.

FARTHER AND FARTHER,
HE'LL BE GOING
FARTHER AND FARTHER DOWN THE WAY
FARTHER AND FARTHER
GONE ON DOWN THE WAY
LORD, GIVE HIM GOOD COMPANY, CAUSE
HE WON'T BE HOME AGAIN TODAY.

End of Play

Part 2

A Battle in the Wilderness

(Late Summer, 1862. Around twelve noon.)

(A wooded area in the South.)

(Pretty much in the middle of nowhere.)

(The **COLONEL** *sings "Passing the Time," and modestly accompanies himself on a banjo.)*

(His Union prisoner, **SMITH**, *is captive in a makeshift wooden cage.)*

COLONEL.

> I'VE SAT ON A MOUNTAIN I'VE SAT ON A HILL
> I LOVE GOD AND COUNTRY, I PAY ALL MY BILLS.
> I'M A PRETTY GOOD HUSBAND, THOUGH DON'T ASK MY
>   WIFE
> IF SHE CATCHES ME HERE, I'LL PAY WITH MY LIFE.
>
> THEY MADE ME A COLONEL, GOT ME A WHITE HORSE
> UPSTANDING, DISTINGUISHED, WITH SERVANTS OF COURSE.
> THE GREY AND THE BLUE AND THE DEAD AND THE BRAVE
> ALL HOPING TO GET BACK HOME ONE OF THESE DAYS.
>
> YES, I'VE TOLD YOU ONCE AND I'LL TELL YOU AGAIN
> I'VE DRUNK ALL YOUR BEER AND I'VE DRUNK ALL YOUR GIN
> I'VE HAD ALL YOUR WHISKEY AND I'VE DOWNED ALL YOUR
>   WINE
> JUST SITTING HERE LONESOME AND PASSING THE TIME.

> *(The* **COLONEL** *stops singing.)*

COLONEL.

You're not singing. I taught you the tune. Taught you the words. You don't recall them?

SMITH.

I recall the words fine. It's hot.

(Cannon fire in the distance.)

(The **COLONEL** *directs* **SMITH** *to move the cage to a shady spot.)*

(After **SMITH** *completes this task he's allowed to remain outside.)*

(Cannon fire in the distance.)

(The singing continues:)

COLONEL.

THIS WAR, IT'S A FIERCE ONE THERE'S BATTLES THERE'S
    CANNONS
COLD FOOD AND COLD TENTS AND A FEAR OF THE FAMINE.
THEY MIGHT CATCH YOU OR SHOOT YOU OR GIVE YOU
    THE POX
AND THE WAY YOU COME HOME MIGHT JUST BE IN A BOX.

Sing with me.

WE GOT A HANDFUL OF BRAVE ONES AND A HANDFUL OF
    COWARDS
WE GOT A YANKEE, SMELLING ROTTEN, AND NEEDING A
    SHOWER.
WE WON'T DIE IN THESE WOODS, WE'LL SURELY FIND OUR
    WAY BACK
AND GIVE OLD MR. LINCOLN ONE HELL OF A WHACK.

COLONEL & SMITH.

I'VE TOLD YOU ONCE AND I'LL TELL YOU AGAIN
I'VE DRUNK ALL YOUR BEER AND I'VE DRUNK ALL YOUR GIN
I'VE HAD ALL YOUR WHISKEY AND I'VE DOWNED ALL YOUR
    WINE
JUST SITTING HERE LONESOME AND PASSING THE TIME.

SMITH.

I'VE WANDERED THE MOUNTAINS AND I'VE WANDERED THE
    HILLS
NOW I HEAR THE BIG GUNS AND THE SOUND GIVES ME
    CHILLS.

I'M BEING HELD PRISONER BY A DRUNKEN DUMB JEB
WHEN I GET MY FREEDOM I'LL CUT OFF HIS HEAD.*

COLONEL.

Changing the words is not polite. Dirty-wounded-flea-bitten-pus-oozing Yankee. I should have left you in the field for dead. Your own Regiment left you. I should have left you too. Let you die there. Instead I carried you along with me. Into this shady grove.

SMITH.

Where I'll bleed to death.

COLONEL.

You were shot in the leg not in the head. And it's nicely bandaged. You'll live.

(Cannon fire in the distance.)

COLONEL.

Those cannons can't be more than 10 miles away. I'll be able to deliver us back to the Regiment before nightfall. What a fool I was for straggling off. My fit of pique. Then we got lost. Horse died. Bad luck. Had to walk. But then I find you, left for dead, a Union Captain, a prize. When I get back and show them my prisoner! My captive Union Captain—well, there will be a hell for me to pay, but when I come back leading you by the scruff of the neck I'll get a wonderful thanks for it.

SMITH.

I'm just a Captain.

COLONEL.

You're an officer in the Union Army. You're a white man. Lucky you're not a Union nigger. If you were, I'd be obligated to shoot you on the spot. (An obligation that's not in any book, not written down, history would find it barbaric, so we keep it unspoken we don't speak

---

*The original lyrics, as taught to Smith by the Colonel are: "I'm being held prisoner / My leg's bleeding red! / I'm lucky he found me. I'd been left for dead."

of it we just shoot on sight.) Lucky for him that he's worth something more than money. Yes and you're worth something alive even though you are just a Captain—

SMITH.

—Just a Captain.

(Rest)

If I was a Major, you'd get more than a thanks, you'd probably get a medal for me. That's how the Union would work it anyhow.

COLONEL.

We reward the same way.

SMITH.

What if I was a Colonel. Or a General.

COLONEL.

If you were a General I would get a promotion.

SMITH.

If you'd caught a General you'd get the moon and they'd cover you over with stars and you'd get a golden goblet from General Robert Edward Lee's own house, a golden goblet for you and your wife both.

COLONEL.

One for me and one for my wife, hand-delivered by General Lee's best nigger.

SMITH.

Yes. Maybe. And you'd get plenty of money. And you'd get more land. If I was a General they'd make you the richest man in the state.

COLONEL.

They'd give me all the land I wanted and without a bald spot on it. Every inch of it, just as green as you please. And 10 teams of mules that don't kick too much.

SMITH.

You'd get 10 teams of mules that don't kick at all.

COLONEL.

And I'd get a mistress. Who is kind. And a little wild. If you were a General I'd get mistress.

SMITH.

But I'm just a Captain.

COLONEL.

Yes. That's a shame.

(Cannons in the distance.)

SMITH.

Ours or yours, you think?

COLONEL.

Ours. Certainly ours.

SMITH.

You sure?

COLONEL.

I'm a Colonel. I'm sure.

(Rest)

You're a Captain serving in the 1st Kansas Colored Infantry. What's it like leading them?

SMITH.

It's like leading anyone else, I suppose.

COLONEL.

You've had experience leading whites?

SMITH.

No.

COLONEL.

Then you can only suppose that your experience is similar. Your Coloreds, left you for dead in the field.

SMITH.

I suppose I looked dead. The men in my command are good men. Hardworking. Brave. They do what I tell them.

COLONEL.

They do what you tell them to do, they're hardworking, they're brave, have you ever wanted to own them?

SMITH.

No.

COLONEL.

I'm not asking you to imagine owning a whole field-full but just one have you ever had the desire to own. Own. Own one just one of them?

SMITH.

No.

COLONEL.

Not a one?

SMITH.

No.

COLONEL.

COLONEL.

COLONEL.

I had a son. He died. At an early age. You remind me of him. The way he would disobey me.

(*Cannon fire in the distance.*)

COLONEL.

Drink with me at least. I don't have much left but I'm courteous enough to share it.

SMITH.

I couldn't.

COLONEL.

I insist. As your captor I insist.

SMITH.

I'm a sober man.

COLONEL.

A sober man and a slaveless man. Living your life with neither bottle nor slave. When you get back home and

I'm guessing you will, they may have to remove your leg but you'll live. You'll get married, I'm guessing you're not already and you'll have your children, I'm guessing you don't have any yet, not even a bastard, your kind don't have bastards, everything your kind do is legitimate, you'll live out your life, with one leg, though, don't forget the one-legged part of it, and on your dying bed surrounded by loved ones, you'll have two private thoughts just before the great blanket covers your head just before the Great Master puts his big hand over your face. First: I should have indulged in spirits, hit the bottle just a little and your second dying-bed thought would be: I should have owned one of them. A darkie. Just one. Just for a day. Just for the feel of it. Because there's nothing like it.

SMITH.

How many do you own?

COLONEL.

Me? A hundred. And would I add to that number? No. Because there's no need to. "Reason not the need"! Oh, hell yes, I most certainly would add to my hundred slaves because it's the mark of a fine man to own them and one can't have too many.

SMITH.

Huh.

(Rest)

We captured a Jeb awhile back. He didn't own any slaves but he'd been promised 10 for his service. "10 is a good number," he kept saying. He didn't have a dollar to his name. He signed up for the war in another man's place, see, there was a rich man, who had been called up to serve, and, the rich man didn't want to come to the War so he got this poor fellah to come in his stead. Said he'd give him 10 slaves for his trouble when he got home. The fellah was pretty excited about the prospect. "10 is a good number," he kept saying. He had the promise-paper in his pocket and he'd show it to our Colonel every chance he got.

COLONEL.

You told that story already.

SMITH.

Did I?

COLONEL.

You've got a fever.

SMITH.

A bit. Hell, I'm alright. I'm fine. The sun makes it hot.

COLONEL.

Drink. Water.

SMITH.

Thank you.

(Rest)

"10s a good number," our prisoner kept saying.

COLONEL.

10 times 10 is a better number. You're wondering what it would be like.

SMITH.

Not at all. I'm a Yankee through and through. Even if I took off my blue coat I'd still be a Yankee. Even if you made me swear to the Rebel Cause I'd still be full of my Yankee blood and my Yankee ways and notions. Even if I came down here to live even if I lived down here for a hundred years and had a hundred slaves I'd still be a Yankee.

COLONEL.

Underneath your blue coat you and me are more alike than different. And I know you are looking at me and you're thinking that it's only a matter of time before we see things your way and we are looking at you and thinking the same thing.

SMITH.

We don't want to change you, we just want to whup you.

COLONEL.

You won't. Ever. Because deep down you think like we think. Agree with me.

SMITH.

SMITH.

COLONEL.

You're from one of those aristocratic families, aren't you? One of those wealthy elite groups in that New York City or Philadelphia? Your daddy's a rich man? He is, isn't he? And you were brought up with a silver spoon in your mouth. Well, I was brought up with a wooden spoon in mine. Self-made. But not you, am I right? Tell me. That would be something, wouldn't it? We'd get your likeness in the newspapers. We'd ask for a ransom. You'd be a prize prisoner. A real prize.

SMITH.

I'm not.

(Cannons fire in the distance.)

SMITH.

(Rest)

You aren't scared I'll run off?

COLONEL.

You can't hardly walk.

SMITH.

I'm a wiley Yankee. You'd best keep your eye on me.

COLONEL.

And I'm a "dumb drunk Jeb" with a loaded pistol.

SMITH.

You best keep me close. Closer than did your man-servant. He's run off, isn't he? I didn't want to mention it, but you sent him to collect wood and water and that was a good hour ago. He's run off.

COLONEL.

He's not run off.

SMITH.

I don't see him around here.

COLONEL.

He's collecting wood and water. I "collected" the rabbits. He's collecting the wood and the water.

SMITH.

He's run off. You got to keep them close or they'll run off.

COLONEL.

Your niggers ever run off?

SMITH.

I don't got none.

COLONEL.

Your soldiers. In your command.

SMITH.

We got deserters and stragglers just like everybody else but it's different. Even if they do leave the Regiment they're not escaping like yours did. Maybe you should go look for him. It was more than an hour ago. You come walking in here and him following behind with those rabbits and then you telling him "go fetch wood and water," and off he went. I bet when you get reunited back with your Regiment, your General's gonna be looking at you. And he'll be looking at me. You'll lead me in by the scruff of the neck, just like you plan to, and your General will be reaching for a medal to give you. Shoot, he'll be taking a medal off his own coat to give you that's how impressed he'll be with your prisoner. And then! He'll notice. That your valet is no longer with you. Hero, you call him. Hero is nowhere to be seen. Hero has misplaced himself. Oh dear. Oh, he'll still give you the medal all right but all the fellahs will be snickering at you behind your back.

COLONEL.

Get back in your pen.

SMITH.

Walking around, getting fresh air made my tongue wag like a dog's backside.

(The **COLONEL** *considers shooting, but instead he kicks* **SMITH** *in his wounded leg.)*

COLONEL.

You're worth more alive than you are dead. Plus one doesn't want to waste the ammunition.

*(***SMITH*** retreats to his cage and the* **COLONEL** *locks him in.)*

COLONEL.

You might have commanded them but I own them. And because I own them I have an understanding of them that you don't have and never will. Hero knows his worth to the penny, and, well, the poor thing is honest. Meaning he won't run off not now not ever. He told me one day: "Master," he said, "running off, well, that would be the same as stealing," he said.

SMITH.

He came to the War with you. He came willingly?

COLONEL.

I asked him to join me and he did so without a second's thought. To get him on board I had to sweeten the pot. I promised him his Freedom.

SMITH.

And you'll keep your word?

COLONEL.

Things these days have grown so very complicated.

SMITH.

You don't intend to keep your word to him.

COLONEL.

I didn't say that.

SMITH.

So if he serves you well, you will keep your promise, yes or no?

COLONEL.

Lucky we found this span of trees. The shade they provide.

(Rest)

Footsteps approaching. Hero!

HERO.

Yes, sir, I'm coming directly.

> *(HERO enters, loaded down with firewood and carrying a bucket of water.)*

COLONEL.

He's returned. What took you so damn long?

HERO.

I was getting a look at the armies coming this way.

COLONEL.

Any scouting that needs scouting I'll do it.

HERO.

Where should I lay it down?

COLONEL.

Just there. Get the fire going so we can eat.

HERO.

Fire's gonna tell them where we are.

COLONEL.

And we'll be reunited all the sooner.

> *(HERO makes the fire.)*

> *(The meat has already been skinned and skewered.)*

HERO.

I seen the Yankees coming. They got a big bunch marching and they're steady on the move. Rebels coming too but not as strong and not as fast and not as many.

SMITH.

How close?

HERO.

SMITH.

COLONEL.

Both sound like they're about 10 miles off.

HERO.

That's what it looks like to me. Both armies headed this way. One coming from one way, one coming from the other.

COLONEL.

Get the supper going.

(**HERO** *lays the skinned rabbits on the fire.*)

HERO.

There ain't plenty of wood out there like you would think. You'd think, us being in the middle of the woods, that there would be plenty of wood. But there ain't.

COLONEL.

You saw them. With your own eyes.

HERO.

I did. You handed me your binoculars so I figured I should use them.

COLONEL.

I'll take them back now.

HERO.

Yankees are marching strong but they're way further off. From what I seen, the Rebels are closer to where we're at.

SMITH.

But the Yankees are marching stronger?

HERO.

SMITH.

COLONEL.

I'll eat something then I'll go and see for myself.

HERO.

You'll catch us up to the Regiment before the day is out, Colonel, just like you say. I know they'll reach us. Or you'll reach them. The world ain't that big a place.

(Rest)

I got the water too. Like you said. Filled the bucket and didn't spill but a little. And all the wood's good and dry.

> *(HERO's got the fire going and the meat cooking.)*

COLONEL.

I'll see to the supper. You'll see to my boots, huh?

> *(HERO helps the COLONEL pull off his boots.)*

> *(The COLONEL minds the fire as HERO shines the boots.)*

COLONEL.

You might as well shine up the Yankee's.

SMITH.

No need for that.

COLONEL.

I want you looking good when I hand you over so hand him your shoes.

SMITH.

I'll wipe them down myself.

COLONEL.

Don't deny me the opportunity of extending my hospitality.

HERO.

I don't mind none.

> *(SMITH hands HERO his boots. HERO then takes off his own boots and works on polishing all three pair.)*

COLONEL.

He's a good worker. You gotta give him that. And trustworthy. I told you he didn't run off. Captain Smith, if you'd of had money you would have wagered

that he'd cut and run and you would have wagered
incorrectly.

SMITH.

Did you run off, Hero?

HERO.

SMITH.

COLONEL.

Go ahead, answer the Yankee. Even though your Master
believes he's one of the devil's minion, you can still talk
to him, Hero, go ahead.

HERO.

No, sir, I didn't run off.

SMITH.

Did you want to?

HERO.

I'm not from around here.

SMITH.

That's a good answer.

COLONEL.

Captain, how much is Hero worth? In dollars and cents.

SMITH.

Your dollars or ours?

COLONEL.

Yours.

SMITH.

I wouldn't know.

COLONEL.

Hazard a guess.

SMITH.

I wouldn't.

COLONEL.

Amuse me.

SMITH.

No thank you.

COLONEL.

Play along.

SMITH.

I said no.

COLONEL.

He's not much fun, is he, Hero?

HERO.

He seems alright.

COLONEL.

But he's ignorant of your worth. So we'll school him. Just for sport. Let's say the Captain guessed 500.

SMITH.

I didn't.

COLONEL.

But we'll say you did. Captain Smith guessed 500 because he doesn't know any better. Major Lewison, Hero, with our Regiment, he says he's got two negras about your size and age and he paid about 500 a piece for them. So common knowledge would say 500.

SMITH.

And common sense would say—

HERO.

Keep quiet. Common sense would say keep quiet.

COLONEL.

Major Lewison would price you at 500. And Lieutenant Beauchamp—

HERO.

The pretty one who's always combing his hair?

COLONEL.

Always talking about his father's thousand acres and thousand slaves. He would set your price lower. 400. But which price is correct? Before the sale was made, a prospective buyer would need to hear a report of your conduct. Hero's a good worker, we've all seen that. He's of the trustworthy type, meaning that he don't run off or stir up trouble. To sum up the report of his conduct, we'll say that Hero minds his Master. That adds an extra hundred or two. If we agreed on the base price as the average of the two prices then we'd be at a price of around 650.

SMITH.

Consider me adequately schooled.

COLONEL.

But we're just getting started.

(Rest)

Now that you've heard of his character it's time to discover if your prospect's got skills. You've got skills don't you, Hero?

HERO.

Farmhand. Valet.

COLONEL.

And as his Master I can vouch for his high competence in both. Now we're at about 700. Skills in blacksmithing?

HERO.

No. You know that already, Colonel. But I could learn it if I had to.

COLONEL.

Blacksmiths go for as much as 2 thousand.

SMITH.

Very informative. And that's enough for me.

COLONEL.

Where are we, Hero?

HERO.

Colonel?

COLONEL.

Are we in the North or the South?

HERO.

We're lost.

COLONEL.

We are lost in the South. Trying to pass the time until our Regiment advances to such a proximity so as we might strike out on foot with the confidence that we will be successful in our efforts to rejoin ourselves to Ourselves. And while we wait. In the heat. We indulge in conversation. Small talk some might call it. But the Yankee, he declines.

(Rest)

> *(He sings a bit more from "Passing the Time.")*

COLONEL.

I'VE BURIED MY FATHER, I'VE BURIED MY SON
WON'T BURY MYSELF THOUGH, WHEN MY LIFE IS DONE.

I tell you what, Captain Smith.

> *(The* **COLONEL** *invites* **SMITH** *to exit the cage.)*

COLONEL.

Play along with us and, if you can, using the information provided, if you can determine Hero's original worth, that is, the price he was when he came to me, then he'll be yours.

HERO.

Just like that.

SMITH.

You'd have your freedom in a heartbeat.

HERO.

Just like that?

COLONEL.

Just like that. Now, just so it's all above board, Hero knows his purchase price so we can't accuse the Colonel of dishonesty should the Captain guess correctly. All right with Smith?

SMITH.

All right with Hero?

HERO.

Alright.

COLONEL.

We'll continue with the inspection.

SMITH.

Go.

COLONEL.

Hardworking, trustworthy. Smart but he'll behave. No skills in reading and writing.

HERO.

COLONEL.

SMITH.

Is that true?

COLONEL.

No more than what I showed him and he and I have agreed that it will always be our secret, how and what he's learned.

HERO.

Yes, sir.

SMITH.

Thereby proving he can keep a secret. I'd say that's worth 100 more. Should I name my price now?

COLONEL.

Not yet not yet. We've made an inspection of his moral character now we will make an inspection of his person. His physical person. Stand.

(**HERO** *stands up.*)

COLONEL.

You got most all your teeth?

HERO.

I believe so.

COLONEL.

But you should never take them at their word.

SMITH.

You said he was trustworthy but you don't trust him?

COLONEL.

Open up your mouth.

> (**HERO** *opens his mouth. The* **COLONEL** *takes a quick glance.*)

COLONEL.

Let the Yankee have a look.

> (**HERO** *moves to where* **SMITH** *can see inside his mouth.*)

SMITH.

Thank you.

COLONEL.

He's got more teeth than me.

SMITH.

So you know two things: he's got his teeth and, as you said before, he's not given to lying.

COLONEL.

And how much is he worth given his skills, his good character and having most all his teeth?

SMITH.

The grand total?

COLONEL.

Yes now's the time let's hear it.

HERO.

SMITH.

COLONEL.

Don't look at Hero. He's not going to tell you with a look. Eyes to the ground, Hero. Now, how much?

SMITH.

I'll say a thousand.

COLONEL.

You're very good.

SMITH.

Am I right?

COLONEL.

Hero how much did I pay for you? Look at the Captain wringing his hands in anticipation or worry. How much, Hero? You know. I know you know. You sneaked a look in my ledger book one day and I knew you did but I didn't whip you for it. You saw how much I paid. How much was it?

SMITH.

A thousand?

HERO.

800.

COLONEL.

Oh. My apologies, Captain.

HERO.

I might be worth a thousand now.

COLONEL.

You came to me 10 years ago. When you were a much younger man. Your price would be lower now.

HERO.

But I've learned things. Skills add to value.

COLONEL.

I see your point. If a man wanted to buy you from me today, how much should I ask for do you think?

HERO.

HERO.

SMITH.

Leave him be. Leave us both be.

COLONEL.

You want me to sit here by myself. In the middle of the wilderness. When we're with the Regiment, and when we're at home, Hero is positively charming. But here, I have to prod him to participate. That does not bode well. It makes me feel—unsettled. Unsettled inside. It makes me forget the promise I made to you, Hero.

HERO.

To figure out my price today, you got to consider whether or—

COLONEL.

Heat or cold, rain or shine, you work just as hard.

HERO.

Whether or not you'll win the War, I meant. The price I'd fetch today would have something to do with that. That's the way I see it.

SMITH.

Good thinking.

COLONEL.

HERO.

COLONEL.

Stand up Hero and undo yourself. We need to finish the inspection.

> (**HERO** *is thinking: Nope.*)

COLONEL.

Undo yourself.

(Rest)

First, we will do a visual inspection and then, we'll do more than just look. As my own father used to say, "Never trust the eye in these 'private' matters. Only trust what your hand will tell you."

(Rest)

Undo yourself, Hero.

HERO.

HERO.

(**HERO** *is thinking: No fucking way.*)

SMITH.

Stop.

COLONEL.

Undo yourself I said.

SMITH.

Stop.

COLONEL.

HERO.

SMITH.

COLONEL.

COLONEL.

Alright. For his sake. We wouldn't want the Yankee to die of fright.

(*The* **COLONEL** *approaches* **HERO** *and, quickly raising his riding crop, he strikes* **HERO** *across the face.*)

COLONEL.

Captain, oh, Captain, how ill-equipped you are for life in the modern world. You're a dying breed.

SMITH.

You don't know anything about us.

COLONEL.

"Us"?

SMITH.

Us Yankees. Us from the North.

COLONEL.

Forgive me, Hero for striking you.

(Rest)

It's been a long day.

(Rest)

A toast to you. A toast to you. Honest, trustworthy, never seen him touch spirits or tobacco, knows his numbers and letters could learn additional trades if necessary, and he's musical. Taught me what little song I manage. A toast to you a toast to you. I'm singing your praises. Here I am, actually singing your praises. Sing with me? The one about toiling?

> *(Cannons fire in the distance.)*

> *(The* **COLONEL** *begins singing "This Bright Wilderness.")*

> **(HERO** *eventually joins in.)*

COLONEL.

IN THE MIDST OF THIS MOST FEARFUL DAY
LET US COUNT OUR MANY BLESSINGS
IN THE MIDST OF THIS BRIGHT WILDERNESS
LET ME SEE THE LIGHT I KNOW.

HERO.

IN THE DARKEST OF THE DARKEST NIGHT
THERE IS STILL A DAY THAT WILL COME ALL RIGHT
GOD IS IN HIS HEAVEN UP ABOVE UP ABOVE
WHILE WE TOIL BRAVELY DOWN BELOW.

> *(Cannons fire.)*

COLONEL.

Take out my plume. Fix it on my hat.

> **(HERO** *takes out a slender box. He removes a large white plume. Suitable for framing.)*

> **(HERO** *affixes the plume on the* **COLONEL**'s *hat. Splendid.)*

COLONEL.

Yankee. What do you think?

SMITH.

You're making an easy target out of yourself.

COLONEL.

Perhaps. I used to wear it all the time. Then only on Sundays and when I had to review the troops. Now I mostly just carry it around in a box. Hero made the box. These days I only wear it in the privacy of my tent. Or in places like this.

The wilderness.

(Rest)

Hero, you have many extraordinary qualities. Were my son living I would want him to be, well—

HERO.

Should I put the feather away?

COLONEL.

Not just yet.

(Cannons fire in the distance.)

COLONEL.

The Yankee thinks I'm a bad person. A bad man. That I'm in the wrong. That I engage, all of us like me, that we engage in bad acts. Constantly. He forgets that I've promised you your Freedom for your Service, isn't that right?

HERO.

You gave your Word on it.

COLONEL.

So I'm not all bad. What will you do once you're free?

(Rest)

HERO.

I couldn't say.

COLONEL.

I know what I would do. I would be sorry to see you go. I would be. And Missus. She would stand on the porch crying and I would put a brave face on it while you went off down the road, heading who knows where to do who knows what, she'd be crying and I'd be standing there wearing my brave face. Once you rounded the bend, out of sight, gone never to return, we'd have supper. Missus crying in her soup and me, making too much conversation. Then would come night fall and we'd be getting ready for bed, Missus would have the bed covers pulled up over her head and I would be sitting on the bed, unable to lie down. Cause I'd be feeling like my good life had left me. Just like I felt when my son died but worse, cause you wouldn't be dead, Hero, you'd just be gone. And I'd weep.

(*The* **COLONEL** *breaks down crying. Real tears.*)

(*Cannons in the distance.*)

(*The* **COLONEL** *regains his composure.*)

COLONEL.

I am grateful every day that God made me white. As a white I stand on the summit and all the other colors reside beneath me, down below. For me, no matter how much money I've got or don't got, if my farm is failing or my horse is dead, if my woman is sour or my child has passed on, I can at least rest in the grace that God made me white. And I don't ever have to fight the Battle of Darkness. What difficulties I may encounter will at least never be those. Life might bring me low but not that low. And I know that I will be received in most any quarter. And if the Lord should choose to further advance my economics, then I will be received in all the great houses. Not so with the lower ones. The lower ones will always be lowly. No matter how high they climb. There is a kind of comfort in that. And I take that comfort. For no matter how low I fall, and no matter how thoroughly I fail, I will always be white.

HERO.

SMITH.

COLONEL.

COLONEL.

Let's put the plume away.

> (**HERO** *removes the plume and places it in the box.*)

SMITH.

Colonel if you were put up on the auction block, what kind of price would you bring, do you think?

COLONEL.

That's a Yankee question.

SMITH.

Clearly as it came out of a Yankee's mouth.

COLONEL.

I'd bring a better price than my negra, I can tell you that.

SMITH.

How come?

COLONEL.

I won't stoop to answer.

HERO.

It's an honest question.

COLONEL.

HERO.

(Rest)

COLONEL.

Things that are worth more bring more money.

SMITH.

And you're worth more.

COLONEL.

Stand up.

SMITH.

You're worth more than him. You're worth more than a Colored? Are you worth more than me?

COLONEL.

Take off his coat and tie his hands. I'm going to shoot you dead. Prepare yourself.

> (HERO *begins to remove* SMITH*'s coat and secure his hands.*)

> (SMITH *is wearing two Union coats. One underneath the other.*)

HERO.

Two coats. How come?

SMITH.

One coat belonged to a dear friend who died.

COLONEL.

Shot by us, most likely.

SMITH.

He was a Private. He died of fever. I wear his coat to keep me warm.

> (*The* COLONEL *aims his gun at* SMITH *who briefly bows his head in prayer. Then:*)

COLONEL.

Ready! Aim! Fire!

> (*But the gun only clicks and the* COLONEL *laughs.*)

COLONEL.

Hero, did you see his eyes? They were as big as two saucer plates. Lock him back up.

> (HERO *returns* SMITH *to his cage. He briefly examines both coats.*)

SMITH.

I appreciate you sparing my life. Even though I'm bleeding to death most likely.

COLONEL.

I'll get a commendation for you.

SMITH.

And now you've also got my thanks. And I'm glad I could give you a laugh.

COLONEL.

Give him back his coats.

(**HERO** *returns the coats. He watches as* **SMITH** *puts them back on.*)

(*Cannons fire in the nearer distance.*)

COLONEL.

You said they were about 10 miles off?

HERO.

The Yankees. Most likely closer now.

COLONEL.

And our Regiment?

HERO.

Closer than that. But not as many.

COLONEL.

HERO.

COLONEL.

I'll go and get a look. You'll watch over the camp.

HERO.

Alright.

COLONEL.

If you all win, their Freedom will come surely. And then what?

(*Cannons in the nearer distance.*)

COLONEL.

Wish me luck.

HERO.

Alright, Boss. Good luck to you.

> *(The **COLONEL** heads out.)*

> *(**HERO** stands at full attention until the **COLONEL** is out of sight.)*

> *(Then he stands "at ease.")*

HERO.

HERO.

HERO.

SMITH.

> *(Rest)*

SMITH.

You can have a seat.

HERO.

I don't need your permission.

> *(Still keeping a wary eye on the prisoner, **HERO** tidies up camp.)*

> *(Cannons in the distance.)*

SMITH.

The cannons. Is it us or them, do you think?

HERO.

I don't think nothing, Boss.

SMITH.

I'm not Boss to you.

HERO.

Alright.

SMITH.

You're Hero? My name's Smith.

(**SMITH** *extends his hand.*)

HERO.

All right.

(Rest)

We don't need to shake hands.

SMITH.

It's courtesy when two men say hello.

HERO.

You're a Yankee prisoner in a wooden cage.

SMITH.

Yes I am.

HERO.

You might die before the night's out.

SMITH.

I might.

HERO.

SMITH.

HERO.

You got children?

SMITH.

Not as yet. You?

HERO.

No. Not yet.

SMITH.

If I had children I may not have signed up. Children make a man cautious.

HERO.

Children make a man brave, seems to me.

SMITH.

As long as I can get back home with both my arms still working good.

HERO.

I was thinking I'd want to have my legs. I pray for God to keep my legs on me.

SMITH.

I pray for arms. Especially with my leg shot up. I'll get home and hug my mother close. I'd need arms for that. I used to pray for legs too but there's probably a limit to what you can get so I'll be satisfied with just my arms. One leg's not so bad. And they got those wheeled chairs that would help me get around.

HERO.

You're right. There probably is a limit. So I'd want my legs. Although Colonel says that the Book says that He is a limitless God, yeah, it still don't hurt none to be on the safe side and not ask for too much.

SMITH.

I raise my hat to your legs.

HERO.

To your arms.

(Raising their caps, they salute each other.)

HERO.

You know I seen the Colonel sleep in the full sun. But me, I'm a working man. Can't sleep with the sun directly overhead. You rest. Go head. I'm keeping watch.

SMITH.

Shouldn't sleep. Can't.

(Cannons in the distance.)

HERO.

Guess the Union's got good food, warm beds, pretty women visiting.

SMITH.

We sleep on the ground and eat bad.

HERO.

What about that Mr. Grant?

SMITH.

The General?

HERO.

He lives in a big house?

SMITH.

He might but I've never seen it.

HERO.

The Colonel says that General Lee's got a fine house. How many slaves does General Grant got?

SMITH.

I don't think he's got any.

HERO.

He's a rich man, though.

SMITH.

Most likely. What I know surely is he's smart. Crafty. Thinks circles around everybody. He once snuck into a Rebel camp and got to know all their ways and snuck out again and they didn't even know he'd been there. And he sneaks up on his own men all the time. That's the key to his strategy.

HERO.

Sneaking up on his own men?

SMITH.

He puts an old coat over his General's gold braid. Hides his medals from sight. Puts on an old cap and maybe some dirt on his face. And he walks around camp or he's sitting by the fire listening to the common soldier in conversation. Getting to know the tenor and the pulse.

HERO.

So he can lead them better.

SMITH.

That's right.

HERO.

And they never figure it's him?

SMITH.

Sometimes, after he's gone. They'll take a count and wonder who the stranger was.

HERO.

And they bust a gut when word gets around that General Ulysses Grant done made a courtesy call. Like a fox in a hen house.

SMITH.

Except he's working to save the hens.

HERO.

You ain't General Ulysses are you?

SMITH.

I'm sure not. Although I do appreciate the question.

HERO.

Cause that would be something, wouldn't it? When we catch back up with them—

SMITH.

Or when they catch back up with us—

HERO.

To have a prize prisoner. But you're just a Captain. With a Private's coat underneath.

SMITH.

What rank are you?

HERO.

They don't give me no rank. I'm just the Colonel's Hero. I'll get my reward if I make it through.

(Rest)

What about that fellah you all caught, the one who says he's getting the ten slaves for his service?

SMITH.

He died.

HERO.

Huh.

SMITH.

The Colonel, he really owns 100 people?

HERO.

More like 10. He's only got 10 of us. He works us like 100, but we're only 10. He likes to talk big.

(Rest)

You talk like a Captain. So I guess you must be one.

SMITH.

HERO.

(Cannons in the distance.)

HERO.

2 coats you got. And that Captain's coat you're wearing over top is too big. The Private's coat is the one that fits you.

(Rest)

You a Private?

SMITH.

—. Yes.

HERO.

Huh.

SMITH.

It was my Captain who died. On the battlefield. When it got dark it got cold. I put his coat on over mine to keep warm.

HERO.

You're a Private serving in the 1st Kansas Colored Infantry.

SMITH.

That's right.

HERO.

The 1st Kansas Coloreds they got Coloreds as Privates.

SMITH.

That's right.

HERO.

SMITH.

HERO.

HERO.

You a Colored man?

SMITH.

Yes.

HERO. *(Aside)*

I'll be damned. I've seen some before that don't look it. He's one of them. Well, I'll be damned.

SMITH.

Does your Colonel know?

HERO.

Hell no.

> (**SMITH** *again extends his hand for a handshake.*)

> (*A more possible moment now.*)

HERO.

What's it like, carrying a gun, having a Regiment?

SMITH.

It's an honor. A big feeling that's hard to put into words.

HERO.

You can stand up straight when you think about it.

SMITH.

That's exactly right.

HERO.

You think you all will beat the Jebs?

SMITH.

God willing. And then the whole world will change. You'll be able to have your own farm. Or you'll move North. Or anything you want.

HERO.

You're really Colored?

SMITH.

I could pass. Yeah. Get myself more money, better rank. Plenty like me who can, they do it. But that's not me.

(**SMITH** *shows* **HERO** *a mark on his forearm.*)

SMITH.

My old Master, he branded each and every one of us.

HERO.

To tell the world you belonged to him.

SMITH.

In case we ran off.

(**HERO** *releases* **SMITH** *from the cage.*)

HERO.

Did you?

SMITH.

Never.

HERO.

Thought about it.

SMITH.

Sure. Plenty.

(**HERO** *shows* **SMITH** *a mark on his neck.*)

HERO.

Boss-Master branded us too. Right here. That and lots of other things.

(Rest)

What kind of price you fetch these days?

SMITH.

I got my freedom handed to me when the Master died. But, if I remember right, I was worth about the same as you.

HERO.

And Freedom might be coming.

SMITH.

It'll come. One way or another, it'll come.

HERO.

How much you think we're gonna be worth when Freedom comes? What kind of price we gonna fetch then?

SMITH.

We won't have a price. Just like they don't. That'll be the beauty of it.

HERO.

Where's the beauty in not being worth nothing?

SMITH.

We won't be able to be moved around, beaten, bought or sold, forced to work and make men rich while we stay poor.

HERO.

Most soldiers they're poor, Colored and White both.

SMITH.

There's more to Freedom than I can explain, but believe me it's like living in Glory.

HERO.

Who will I belong to?

SMITH.

You'll belong to yourself.

HERO.

So—when a Patroller comes up to me, when I'm walking down the road to work or to what-have-you and a Patroller comes up to me and says, "Whose nigger are you, Nigger?" I'm gonna say, "I belong to myself"? Today I can say, "I belong to the Colonel."

*(Imagining being confronted by a Patroller, **HERO** holds up his hands. Reminiscent of: "Hands up! Don't shoot!")*

HERO.

"I belong to the Colonel," I says now. That's how come they don't beat me. But when Freedom comes and they stop me and ask and I say, "I'm my own. I'm on my own and I own my ownself," you think they'll leave me be?

SMITH.

I don't know.

HERO.

Seems like the worth of a Colored man, once he's made Free, is less than his worth when he's a slave.

SMITH.

Is that how come you don't run off?

HERO.

Maybe. I'm worth something so me running off would be like stealing.

SMITH.

Seems to me you got a right to steal yourself.

HERO.

Maybe. Maybe not.

SMITH.

How about you try on my coat. Go ahead. Try it on.

HERO.

A Union Army coat in the rank of Captain.

SMITH.

Try it on. I won't tell no one you wore it. Go ahead.

*(After a quick glance ensuring that the coast is clear, **HERO** hurriedly tries on **SMITH**'s extra coat.)*

SMITH.

Looks good on you.

HERO.

Feels good. Don't know if it's the Captain part or the Union part. Probably some of both.

(Rest)

You know what I call the Colonel behind his back? I call him "Peacock."

SMITH.

"Colonel Peacock"?

HERO.

No, just "Peacock." Him and that fool bird-wing feather in his cap that he loves so much. "Peacock."

(Rest)

Sometimes I think there's a broke part of me inside. Snapped in two. Huh.

(Rest)

The Colonel, he says, "Get over here, Hero, and do this and that." And I say, "Yes, sir," out loud but to myself I say, "Sure thing, Peacock, sure thing, Peacock." Sometimes he wonders why I'm smiling and that's how come.

SMITH.

"Peacock." That's good. Huh. Hero's a good name.

HERO.

Colonel named me that. Master before him only called me Joe. Who named you Smith?

SMITH.

It was my father's name. If you could name yourself anything what would you be?

HERO.

HERO.

(Rest)

HERO.

That's a big question. I don't rightly know.

SMITH.

Both of us. Satisfied with the names they gave. Huh. This world is such a mess. How's a Colored gonna make his way? Seems like we either get sold off by somebody or sell out our ownselves. You could be bought and sold and so could I.

HERO.

That'll end with Freedom.

SMITH.

But what if it don't somehow? Sometimes I get the feeling that the heart of the thing won't change easy or quick. Cause of the way we were bought and brought over here in the first place. Maybe even with Freedom, that mark, huh, that mark of the marketplace, it will always be on us. And so maybe we will always be twisting and turning ourselves into something that is going to bring the best price. That's the way we were born into this, so is it always gonna be like that for us, slavery or not? Freedom or not? Are we ever going to get us a better place in the marketplace?

HERO.

You're talking like you wanna burn something down.

SMITH.

I'm just saying: if you say you're broke, I say you're double-broke—snapped in two without a penny to your name and hoping someone'll pay more than 800 dollars for you, but goddamnit, God willing, some day we'll have a place besides just the auction block. And maybe that starts by stealing yourself. Stealing yourself, making yourself like metal on the inside. Maybe it'll get better from there. But, I don't know.

(*Cannons sound in the near distance.*)

HERO.

Footsteps. Someone's coming. Take back your coat.

(**HERO** *returns the coat.* **SMITH** *returns to the cage.*)

(*As someone approaches the camp* **HERO** *draws his knife.*)

(**HERO** *rushes toward the approaching figure, knife drawn.*)

COLONEL.

Hero!

HERO.

Yes?

COLONEL.

It's only me.

HERO.

Colonel.

COLONEL.

Knife drawn. Put it away. God. I should have called out to you as I came up but I didn't think—

HERO.

The sun's in my eyes. And the heat.

COLONEL.

Put your knife away.

COLONEL.

HERO.

(**HERO** *puts away his knife.*)

SMITH.

You saw them. Coming this way.

COLONEL.

Hero, pack up the camp.

(**HERO** *begins to pack up the camp.*)

COLONEL.

If we move quickly we'll be able to catch up to our Regiment. They're not as great in number as they were when we left them. They'll welcome us. We'll have to move quickly.

SMITH.

The Union Army's closer, aren't they?

> *(The* **COLONEL** *rapidly removes* **SMITH** *from his cage, tying a thick rope around his neck.)*

COLONEL.

Hero. Take hold of this rope and lead the Yankee along. With his leg he won't be able to move as fast as you so carry him if you have to. I'll head out and find us the quickest way. And if he tries to run off, you call out to me and I'll shoot him dead, you hear?

HERO.

He won't run. I'll see to it.

COLONEL.

I trust you will.

COLONEL.

HERO.

SMITH.

COLONEL.

HERO.

We'll follow behind.

COLONEL.

God Bless.

> *(The* **COLONEL** *heads out quickly.)*

> *(They watch the* **COLONEL** *move out of sight.)*

> *(***HERO** *holds tightly to the rope fastened securely around* **SMITH** *'s neck.)*

HERO.

SMITH.

HERO.

SMITH.

SMITH.

Let's go. We don't want to fall too far behind him.

HERO.

SMITH.

(Rest)

    *(**HERO** unties the rope from **SMITH**'s neck.)*

HERO.

I don't know if I'm qualified to give freedom to another man seeing as how I'm not a free man myself but I give it to you just the same. God willing I'll make up for a horrible wrong I did.

SMITH.

What kind of wrong?

HERO.

No matter. If you're lucky you could move down the hill some, lay low for a spell, then join back up with your fellahs.

SMITH.

How you gonna explain me being gone?

HERO.

I'll think of something. Not to worry.

SMITH.

HERO.

    *(**SMITH** quickly removes his Private's uniform coat.)*

SMITH.

You're coming with me. Put it on.

    *(**HERO** just holds the coat.)*

SMITH.

Raise your right hand and solemnly swear.

HERO.

I swear.

SMITH.

Well done. You're a Union Soldier now. A Private in the 1st Kansas Coloreds. Come on.

*(**SMITH** moves to leave. **HERO** doesn't follow.)*

HERO.

HERO.

SMITH.

Come on!

(Cannon fire in the very near distance. Rumble in the earth, fire and danger in the air.)

SMITH.

Come on!

*(**SMITH** tries to pull **HERO** along. No luck.)*

SMITH.

HERO.

SMITH.

HERO.

(A parting embrace.)

*(**SMITH** heads northward, toward the safety of the oncoming Union Army.)*

(It's doubtful that he'll make it.)

HERO.

HERO.

HERO.

*(**HERO** removes his Confederate uniform coat.)*

(He puts on the Union coat.)

HERO.

HERO.

HERO.

(Then he replaces the grey army coat, pulling it over the blue one.)

(And Hero heads southward, taking the path the Colonel took, back toward the heart of the Rebel Army stronghold.)

(The MUSICIAN *sings:)*

THIS BRIGHT WILDERNESS (REPRISE)

IN THE MIDST OF THIS MOST FEARFUL DAY
LET US COUNT OUR MANY BLESSINGS
IN THE MIDST OF THIS BRIGHT WILDERNESS
LET ME SEE A LIGHT I KNOW.

IN THE DARKEST OF THE DARKEST NIGHT
THERE IS STILL A DAY THAT COMES ALL RIGHT:

GOD IS IN HIS HEAVEN
UP ABOVE UP ABOVE
WHILE WE TOIL
BRAVELY DOWN BELOW.

WHEN THE ROAD IS LONG AND THE EYE IS WEAK
LET US HOPE THE HEART IS MERRY.
LET US KEEP ON KEEPING ON, YOU KNOW.
LET US CHERISH ALL WE CARRY.

WHEN THE THICK IS THIN AND THE PLENTY ENDS
IT WILL BE AS IT HAS ALWAYS BEEN:

GOD IS IN HIS HEAVEN
UP ABOVE UP ABOVE
WHILE WE TOIL
BRAVELY DOWN BELOW.

GOD IS IN HIS HEAVEN
UP ABOVE UP ABOVE
WHILE WE TOIL
BRAVELY DOWN BELOW.

End of Play

Part 3

The Union of My
Confederate Parts

(The **MUSICIAN** *sings:)*

MISPLACED MYSELF

THEY BE LOOKING HIGH AND LOW
THEY BE LOOKING IN THE TREES
THEY BE SEARCHING ON THE RIVERS
THEY BE QUESTIONING THE BEES.

I'M LONG GONE
I AIN'T SITTING ON YOUR SHELF
I HAVE MISPLACED MYSELF
I HAVE MISPLACED MYSELF.

I AIN'T WORKING IN YOUR FIELD
I AIN'T MINDING IN YOUR STORE
I AIN'T CHURNING UP YOUR BUTTER
YOU DON'T MATTER ANYMORE.

I'M LONG GONE
I'VE SKIPPED TOWN WITH ALL YOUR WEALTH
I HAVE MISPLACED MYSELF
I HAVE MISPLACED MYSELF.

AND OH, I KNOW YOU BE MISSING ME
AND OH, HERE I GO:
SAILING FAR FROM THE DEVIL CROSS THE DEEP BLUE SEA.

I AIN'T LEAVING YOU NO TRAIL
I DONE WENT AND BROKE MY CHAIN
YOU GOT EVERYTHING TO LOSE
I'VE GOT EVERYTHING TO GAIN.

I'M LONG GONE
I AIN'T SITTING ON YOUR SHELF
I HAVE MISPLACED MYSELF
I HAVE MISPLACED MYSELF.

(Fall, 1863. Far West Texas. A slave cabin in the middle of nowhere.)

(Late in the afternoon, about an hour before sunset.)

(THE RUNAWAY SLAVES *huddle together on the porch.)*

THIRD RUNAWAY.

Do you think she'll dream again tonight?

SECOND RUNAWAY.

What difference does it make? Who is she to us?

FIRST RUNAWAY.

She fed us. 3 good meals. No questions asked.

SECOND RUNAWAY.

No questions cause it's dangerous for them to know our business. Runaways like we are. The less they know the less they can be made to tell.

FIRST RUNAWAY.

Penny: she's a good cook. And Homer: "the man who's got the land written down in his mind," he's out in the field right now. While we sit here, he's stealing from his Missus' crops so we'll have food when we head out.

SECOND RUNAWAY.

We don't need to get too deep with them is all I mean. The little we already know of them is more than plenty. As things stand, it's safer that way.

FIRST RUNAWAY.

Ok ok.

THIRD RUNAWAY.

Still and all: I can wonder. And I wonder if she'll dream again tonight. I wonder what she dreams of.

FIRST RUNAWAY.

> Her husband, Hero, that's clear enough cause she calls
> out his name.

THIRD RUNAWAY.

> But what of him? Must be horrible. The way she wakes
> up screaming. And running from the cabin. And
> Homer hurrying out behind her. And the way he has to
> hold her close. And cover up her mouth.

SECOND RUNAWAY.

> Lucky for us, by nightfall we'll be gone on our way, so
> at midnight, if she does dream and scream, we'll be too
> far gone to hear her.

THIRD RUNAWAY.

> And so, what difference does it make you're thinking?
> *(Rest)*
> We came here figuring Homer would run off with us
> right away but he said no. Why you think that is?

FIRST RUNAWAY.

> Because of his foot. He's lost his foot and his
> confidence.

THIRD RUNAWAY.

> It ain't that. It's Penny, she's rooted here. And Homer
> is rooted to her.

FIRST RUNAWAY.

> Which makes her something to us.

THIRD RUNAWAY.

> Tru dat.

SECOND RUNAWAY.

> Then I say we go on without him. We've come this far.
> We can find our way to freedom on our own all right.

THIRD RUNAWAY.

> We can kinda-sorta.

FIRST RUNAWAY.

> We can maybe. Not.

SECOND RUNAWAY.

Our luck's dried up then. It's hopeless. I'll go hang myself from the nearest tree. I'll go cut my own throat. I'll go jump in the river and drown.

THIRD RUNAWAY.

Please. We got a little more than an hour before it's dark enough to jet. That's time enough to get Homer to change his mind.

SECOND RUNAWAY.

Good luck with that.

FIRST RUNAWAY.

We'll work on him together. Mercy. Here he comes.

> *(**HOMER** enters from the fields, carrying a small sack of harvested vegetables. He also carries a newly found stick.)*

THE RUNAWAY SLAVES.

THIRD: "Before I'll be a slave, I'll be buried in my grave."

SECOND: True dat.

FIRST: True dat, right, Homer?

HOMER.

I couldn't say for sure. Truth is a funny thing, you know?

THE RUNAWAY SLAVES.

THIRD: The Truth will set you free.

SECOND: True dat.

FIRST: True dat for sure.

HOMER.

What's for sure is you been running and now you resting. Here's food for your journey. No one saw me and if they did they just thought I was working. Where you all from exactly?

THE RUNAWAY SLAVES.
THE RUNAWAY SLAVES.

HOMER.

What's the use getting friendly if you'll be gone by nightfall? Yeah, ok. Keep me at arm's length and I'll give a good wave goodbye when you go.

THE RUNAWAY SLAVES.

FIRST: I ran from a place east of here.

SECOND: I ran from a place further south.

THIRD: And I ran from a place further south than that.

FIRST: We met up on the road.

SECOND: And now we're running together.

THIRD: Running buddies you could say.

HOMER.

And you're waiting for night before you move on. The moon was gone last night. You shoulda left then.

THE RUNAWAY SLAVES.

FIRST: We were waiting for you.

SECOND: Still are.

THIRD: Say you'll come with.

> (Using the stick, **HOMER** practices writing in the dirt.)

FIRST RUNAWAY.

We're leaving out tonight.

HOMER.

It'll still be safe to travel. The moon will be just a sliver.

FIRST RUNAWAY.

Our best chance is if you come with us.

HOMER.

Things are different now. Changed.

THE RUNAWAY SLAVES.

FIRST: You're still Homer.

SECOND: And we're still here waiting.

THIRD: You know how to read the land and sky.
You can read the weather and the birds.

FIRST: We've got papers.

SECOND: We made them ourselves.

THIRD: Some for you too.

FIRST: Just say the word.

SECOND: Slavery, in a way, it don't got nothing to do with the Master.

THIRD: Remember who you are. Here's your chance to be true.

FIRST: True dat.

SECOND: You'll go tonight with us.

FIRST: Whatchu say, huh?

THIRD: Whatchu say?

HOMER.

You can read and write your letters good. I thank you for teaching me this much. How's this look?

THE RUNAWAY SLAVES.

FIRST, SECOND & THIRD: Looks like you're learning.

THIRD: There's more reading and writing where we're going.

FIRST: Come with us and we'll make it.

SECOND: Won't be easy—

FIRST: But we'll make it. With you we'll make it all the way.

THIRD: "Ain't nobody gonna turn me around."

HOMER.

Don't get ahead of yourselves.

(Rest)

Once I thought I was gonna make it all the way. Just like you. And this porch here is as far as Homer got. There's worse things, though. The last time I ran they cut off my foot.

THE RUNAWAY SLAVES.

THIRD: But you can still walk, can't you?

SECOND: And you can walk good.

FIRST: You will walk away tonight with us.

HOMER.

I don't think so.

THE RUNAWAY SLAVES.

THIRD: Now's your chance.

SECOND: You got runaway blood.

FIRST: Run away and follow that.

HOMER.

Not so fast now.

(Rest)

You know sometimes I sit here thinking about my foot and how I'll grow me another one. Lizards can do that, why not me? We don't work that way. Ok. Things could be worse. I got a good place here. But no foot. I got Penny by my side. But no foot. Penny dreams of Hero. I dream of my foot. Now some letters. Still no foot. There's worse things.

FIRST RUNAWAY.

There's better.

HOMER.

Such as?

THE RUNAWAY SLAVES.

Freedom.

HOMER.

I don't know.

FIRST RUNAWAY.

Then stay.

THIRD RUNAWAY.

And rot.

HOMER.

I can't leave Penny.

THIRD RUNAWAY.

Because of love?

HOMER.

Because of work.

FIRST & SECOND RUNAWAY.

Please.

HOMER.

Wouldn't be fair to leave her here all alone with the Missus.

THIRD RUNAWAY.

Hero might be coming home soon, the way she dreams of him, wouldn't you say? Or is that just the way I'm reading it?

HOMER.

She dreams about him in a way that makes me think that he's close by. But dead or living, I don't know.

SECOND RUNAWAY.

If he's living, and if he should come home, better for you to be long gone, don't you think?

HOMER.

I've made my peace with Hero. What he owes me I can't never get back. And what do I want to take the place of my foot? Not this place, no. But, huh, a new place could be just the thing. To run and to make it to Freedom. To do the thing I always said I'd do. That

would show him. I'd show him by being long gone.
That'd be something. It'd be funny. I'd be laughing.
And Hero, oh he just might laugh. In the even-ing-out
of things, he just might see the humor in it.

THIRD RUNAWAY.

So you'll go?

HOMER.

(Rest)

I'll go. Lord help me I will.

THE RUNAWAY SLAVES.

Good.

THIRD RUNAWAY.

And Penny?

FIRST RUNAWAY.

Maybe she'll come too.

THIRD RUNAWAY.

It would be a joy to you if she did.

SECOND RUNAWAY.

And happy men got a spring in they step.

THIRD RUNAWAY.

You wouldn't be looking back over your shoulder and
thinking of her.

FIRST RUNAWAY.

And that would be a help as we move forward.

HOMER.

Penny will stay. We're foolish thinking that her mind
will change. What that gal does is her own doing. Not
mine. And don't you worry, I won't be waving goodbye
any longer than necessary.

(Rest)

Penny, she don't got eyes for me. Not ears neither. All
she sees and hears is Hero coming down the road, even
though he ain't coming. She's a true wife to Hero if
there ever was. And it's not like she's on my mind no
way no how. Hell, I'm going with you. That's for sure.
Leave all this behind.

(**HOMER** *continues practicing his letters in the dirt.*)

THE RUNAWAY SLAVES.

THIRD: I made a choice one morning
   Between the ones I loved
   And the thing I loved more than them.

SECOND: They say you shouldn't love things
   More than people.
   They say that things,
   Things come and go.

FIRST: But people, people, they come and go too.

THIRD: Too true that.

SECOND: Too true that.

THIRD: I loved my mother. Left her behind.

FIRST: I loved my brother. He died.

SECOND: I loved my sister. She was afraid of the dark.

FIRST: I loved Master, in a way, and he, he left his mark.
   He did right by law but wrong by me.

THIRD: Penny, she does right by law, but wrong by you.

SECOND: Strange thing to love someone who does you
   wrong. Even if they do you wrong by doing right.

FIRST: You don't care for her, so you say, but "Penny."

THIRD: The only word you wanna write.
   "Penny" in the dirt. "Penny."

SECOND: Over and over and over.

(**HOMER** *glances down the road then back to his writing.*)

HOMER.

   It's just a word. One of many. She's just a gal. Nothing
   more than that. She ain't mine.

THE RUNAWAY SLAVES.

Even so.

HOMER.

Even so nothing. She ain't tied to me. My foot weren't tied to me. And I ain't tied to this place. So I'm going. To my Freedom. True dat.

(**PENNY** *comes in carrying a bag of seeds.*)

PENNY.

How long have you been looking down the road for me, Homer?

HOMER.

Not at all. We've been busy.

PENNY.

Tell the truth. Scratching in the dirt with that stick.

HOMER.

I was worried. Patrollers on the road. Sundown will be here soon.

PENNY.

There's still plenty of daylight and folks know I work for Missus. I can share some of this with you all. Missus won't miss a few handfuls. And don't worry, I was up at the house all day but I didn't do or say nothing to give you away.

THE RUNAWAY SLAVES.

FIRST: We're grateful.

SECOND: We thank you.

THIRD: When a good man thinks of love he thinks of you.

HOMER.

Bad news? You got trouble on your mind. I can see.

PENNY.

What's that scratching say?

HOMER.

It says everything.

PENNY.

"Everything." Is that how you write it? Looks pretty.

HOMER.

PENNY.

HOMER.

Kiss?

PENNY.

Homer.

HOMER.

No harm in asking.

PENNY.

Because you like the sound of no.

HOMER.

There's a yes in that no. Curled up inside somewhere. Kiss.

PENNY.

Tell me: whatcha think of my dreams? I dreamed true about Hero's dog: that his dog returned to him in the War. And months later Missus heard the same news in a letter from her Colonel.

HOMER.

That was something. You could make money telling folks if it's gonna rain.

PENNY.

Don't make fun.

HOMER.

I'm not.

THE RUNAWAY SLAVES.

FIRST: A skill like yours is a kind of reading.

SECOND: You're reading a page that ain't wrote yet.

THIRD: You got value that would be better spent in a better place.

PENNY.

You think?

(Rest)

Up at the house, just now, there was a letter on the table. Opened up already. And Missus sitting in the kitchen. Fighting back tears. I asked if the letter'd brought news. She looked up to the sky, like she was praying, but no words.

HOMER.

Bad news. What'd she tell you.

PENNY.

At first all she gave me was a look. And this bag of seeds. Nothing else. She told me to get on back here and I went on. I was a good span away when she comes running up after me. When I seen her running I was wanting to run too, but not towards her—you know, she was yelling so I thought she was in one of her whipping moods, so my feet stayed rooted to the spot, figuring if there was blows coming I'd take them then and there cause me running would just fan her fire, you know. She come up to me, face dripping with sweat, hair all which-away. Bending over double to catch her breath. Finally she can speak. The words come quick.

THIRD RUNAWAY.

What's she say?

PENNY.

Mumbling something about a Proclamation or some such.

HOMER.

Proclamation?

FIRST RUNAWAY.

What about?

PENNY.

She was rambling. I couldn't make head or tail of it. "War's still going on," she says. "Proclamation," she says. "Freedom," she says.

THE RUNAWAY SLAVES & HOMER.

"Freedom"?

PENNY.

Then, the clearest part, hollered out, "The Colonel, he's dead," she says. "He's free cause he's dead."

THE RUNAWAY SLAVES.

SECOND: Dead.

FIRST: Dead in the dirt.

THIRD: And your Hero?

HOMER.

What of Hero?

PENNY.

"And that Hero of yours, he's dead too," she says. Hero dead too.

HOMER.

Dead.

THE RUNAWAY SLAVES.

Hero dead.

PENNY.

And then—she hugs me.

(Rest)

She was just that sad.

> (**HOMER** *moves to console* **PENNY,** *but she stops him, keeping him at arm's length.*)

PENNY.

Let me alone with it. Let me alone with it.

(Rest)

There's worse things. I seen it coming: he's dead. There's worse things.

HOMER.

Leave with us tonight.

PENNY.

Leave? Here? With Hero practically home?

HOMER.

He's dead.

PENNY.

Oh. With you saying it somehow I believe it. I couldn't believe it coming from her mouth but I can believe it coming from yours. Just let me alone with it. Can't cry. Not yet. Can't yell. Not today. She can cry. Not me. Gotta save my strength. But for what. Do something. Walk. Work. Move. Flee. Run. Don't think I can outrun it, though. Still can't cry yet. Can't yell yet. Will some day. Not today.

HOMER.

We're heading out tonight. You'll come with us.

(Rest)

I'm leaving with them tonight. You'll come with me. We'll be together.

PENNY.

On the road, hiding from shadows. Cold, hungry, and the Patrollers. What, you want them to catch you and cut off your other foot, or worse?

HOMER.

I'll make sure you're safe. These people are good people. Smart. I know the land. And I'll make sure you don't go hungry and at night, at night, I'll, I'll—and I—I Love You.

PENNY.

HOMER.

(Rest)

PENNY.

What's that say again?

HOMER.

P-E-N-N-Y. It says "Penny."

PENNY.

You're not right somehow. You're a good man, Homer. What you want with a gal like me, I don't know. A married-gal now a widow-gal. You head out with them and get North and get yourself a good job and a nice gal. I still see him so you best start looking at something else.

HOMER.

You won't be sad forever. Maybe some day, a kiss—

PENNY.

No.

HOMER.

You're sad now.

PENNY.

I'll get back to work. He promised he'd come home. And when he comes I'll bury him, if they bring him. I'm ready to move on. But not with them. And not with you.

THE RUNAWAY SLAVES.

FIRST: We'll be leaving soon.

SECOND: And we appreciate your kindness.

THIRD: Homer will guide us and you'll give him your blessing when he goes.

HOMER.

I'd like more than a blessing. How about a kiss? A kiss goodbye, right?

PENNY.

Homer.

HOMER. *(Aside)*

We spent time together. How she can lie down with me but not ever kiss me, I don't know.

PENNY. *(Aside)*

I laid down with him because there was room in my bed. It was empty. But my heart, it's full. No room in there for nothing else.

HOMER.

You're fearful, I'm brave: no matter. I got one foot you got two: no matter.

(Rest)

There's big things and then there's bigger things that small them up, you know? Over where I came from, the sea was so big. But the sky smalled it up. My younger days got smalled up by my years. My one foot gets smalled up by everything. You want to wait, but he's dead and you're scared. Going could small that up.

(Rest)

No better time to leave than tonight. And there's nothing left to do but go.

PENNY.

No.

HOMER.

Then just a kiss, then. A goodbye kiss if not for nothing else.

(PENNY *gently kisses* HOMER.)

(Another kiss. It's love.)

PENNY.

HOMER.

THE RUNAWAY SLAVES.

SECOND: Tied to this place.

FIRST: But the bond is coming loose.
  Loose loose.

SECOND: Another bond comes up
  To take its place.

FIRST: A bond to something better.

THIRD: The weight that keeps her here
  The weight to the dead
  To the past
  That pulls her
  From underneath the ground
  It breaks
  With tears
  That will come some day
  But not tonight
  Tonight
  She'll free herself.
  She can't help it.

PENNY.

I'll go. With you and them. We'll all leave tonight together.

HOMER.

I'll get everything ready. I was just going to go with nothing, but now, with you, you'll need things.

(**HOMER** *goes inside to ready their few things.*)

PENNY.

My Hero's dead. I'm gone.

THE RUNAWAY SLAVES.

FIRST: With you, we'll be a joyful group.

SECOND: We'll travel with speed.

THIRD: We just might make Freedom by morning.

FIRST: You got word that your Hero's dead.

THIRD: You've made a wise choice.

PENNY.

But should I wait? Just to make sure. Cause look, even
now, coming this way, someone—or something.

THE RUNAWAY SLAVES.

Hero?

PENNY.

No, too small for a man, probably just a wild thing.

FIRST RUNAWAY.

A wild thing called Freedom is calling.

Tonight is your best chance

And with nothing to wait for here

Any longer, Penny,

You owe it to you

And to those who will come through after you.

The ones who will come after

The one you're carrying now.

PENNY.

How did you know? I'm not far gone.

THIRD RUNAWAY.

We can read the signs, Penny.

The look in your eye

The lift in your step

The new one will come

You'll piece together the broken parts.

You two will make it new.

True dat.

PENNY.

My child. Me and Homer's.

SECOND RUNAWAY.

You will come with us tonight and wake up in Ohio
Or California even
"Soon to be living in a brand-new state."
Where the sun is always shining.

PENNY.

Help me bear it. Help me bear it. Help me bear it.

THIRD RUNAWAY.

We'll shoulder the burden.

PENNY.

I'm going. True dat. And I'm glad.

> *(An actor as* **ODYSSEY DOG** *comes in. He sees* **PENNY** *and runs around and around her, gently calling her name.)*

ODYSSEY DOG.

Penny! Penny penny penny penny penny.

> *(***PENNY*** *embraces him. He giggles and wiggles then boldly licks her on the face.)*

> *(Hearing the excitement,* **HOMER** *comes outside.)*

PENNY.

Homer! Oddsee Dog is home!

HOMER.

Look at you, boy! Look at you!

ODYSSEY DOG.

Oddsee's home! Oddsee's home! Oddsee's home!

PENNY.

You sure are home, aren't you?

ODYSSEY DOG.

It's true, Penny, it's true. I ran off, nobody could find
me. Hero left. I found Hero. But Hero isn't Hero
anymore. Yep I'm home. Yep. Yep. Yep I got news. I got
news I got news lots to tell happy I'm home good to

see you. So many dead. The Old Man dead. The others dead or sold off. That's sad. Whodat what's that smell? Strangers. New folks. Runaways. Runaways. Woah. Shhh. I won't tell. Good people. Food. Water. Lots of news. Penny's got a baby. Homer's in love. Both ready to jet. Both wondering. Both wondering. Happy to be home.

PENNY.

Get him some water. You must be thirsty. Hungry too.

(**HOMER** *gets* **ODYSSEY DOG** *water and something to eat.*)

HOMER.

Dog's here. Hero ain't. That's plain enough. Them letters the Missus got said the dog wouldn't never leave Hero's side. Now here he is back all alone.

PENNY.

Tell us, Oddsee, how Hero died.

ODYSSEY DOG.

PENNY.

PENNY.

Oddsee?

ODYSSEY DOG.

Penny?

PENNY.

Must be hard for you. Knowing what you know. Tell it.

ODYSSEY DOG.

The War continues on. The details, pretty much unspeakable. Who will win? Who can know?

THE RUNAWAY SLAVES.

THIRD: Win or lose
    Means the same to us
    As long as we're down here.

FIRST: The Union won't reach this land any time soon.

SECOND: Unless the dog knows different.

PENNY.

And what of Hero? Is he dead? I know he's dead. Tell me how he died. I can bear it. Or if by some way he's living, hurry and tell me that.

HOMER.

He's dead. We know. But you tell it. We'll believe it coming from you. Go on.

PENNY.

ODYSSEY DOG.

HOMER.

(Rest)

ODYSSEY DOG. *(Aside)*

This is one of those moments we sometimes find ourselves in. I've got news and they want me to tell it. But the telling is hard because my news will make one sad and the other happy. I don't want to disappoint. It's a hard life when one wants to please. Why does life have to be like this? I'm just a dog.

THE RUNAWAY SLAVES.

FIRST: Hearing how he died will help us.

THIRD: It will help you, Penny, to put him to rest.

SECOND: And our journey will gain speed when you free
         yourself from this place and all that's in it.

HOMER.

Tell it. Go head.

PENNY.

I can bear it. Hero's dead. How'd he die?

ODYSSEY DOG.

It's a long story.

(Rest)

He told me how it was on the day he left. You all remember. The Master gave Hero a uniform of his very own. It was grey from top to bottom.

PENNY.

Oddsee.

HOMER.

Hero's dead, right?

ODYSSEY DOG.

Boss-Master had a hat. And a feather from a bird. And Hero had a pair of boots from the Boss-Master. The boots he had were old. But they were still so nice. So nice, so nice so nice, yep. So nice so pig leather and I so I so wanted to chew on them because they were like the pig that had been slaughtered and dressed and tanned and cut and sewn back together to make those boots, it was like the pig was still alive and you know how I would chase the pigs, when we had pigs to chase. Chewing on those boots would have been my pleasure. But I put my pleasure aside for the honor of walking by my Master's side.

PENNY.

The Master is dead, right?

ODYSSEY DOG.

Which one?

HOMER.

The Boss-Master, the Colonel, you know.

ODYSSEY DOG.

When I say my Master of course I'm speaking of Hero. Him and you all have a Master, but his and you all's Master is not my Master. Although you could say that, because the Boss-Master owns Hero who in turn owns me, you could figure that the Boss-Master is in fact my Master. But he is not. Although, the Great Master, the one who sits in the sky, you know, the Great Master is

Boss-Master's Master and Old-Hero's Master and my
Master too, but that Colonel-Boss-Master is not my
Master. When the Colonel called me, I would never
ever come.

PENNY.

Oddsee. Tell me.

ODYSSEY DOG.

I'm getting to it. Getting home was hard, and what I'm
getting to now is harder.

(Rest)

Old-Hero got me in as a pup, remember? Yep. Yep. Back
then I wasn't much to speak of. Funny eyes. Named me
Oddsee. Funny name. I grew to like it. Funny how you
can grow to like something like that.

HOMER.

Hero's dead. Just say it.

ODYSSEY DOG.

I'm getting to it.

HOMER.

Taking the long way around.

ODYSSEY DOG.

I'm getting to it. I'm getting to it. They told me how
they marched out of here, Old-Hero marching and
the Master riding that white horse named Fortune.
Fortune was prancing. Sounds like it was quite a sight.
And they said, Boss-Master's Missus, she cried as she
waved goodbye and you cried too Penny and Homer
you just waved. Boss-Master said he woulda took you
along but what did the war need with a man with only
one foot, and besides you couldn't be trusted. What
did the Rebels need with a rebel. Huh. Boss-Master was
only going to take Hero because he could be trusted to
stay by the Master's side at all times. Hero, yep, he was
like me in that respect.

HOMER.

Is he alive or dead, dog?

ODYSSEY DOG.

I'm getting to it. Don't kick me. Please.

HOMER.

ODYSSEY DOG.

PENNY.

Go on.

ODYSSEY DOG.

(*Rest*)

Sometimes the day was fine and the sun came out.
Sometimes it rained. Sometimes there was—a mist.

HOMER.

A mist?!

ODYSSEY DOG.

Like at Shiloh and Boss-Master, not Hero you
understand, but Hero's Master, you understand, when
he led a charge on his new Fortune and new Fortune
fell down and the Boss-Master was going along so
fast that I swear the Boss-Master kept charging right
along, long after his new Fortune had fell out from
underneath him. Boss-Master charging alone through
the air.

(*Rest*)

Once there was a house. I forget where. There was a
house with some women in it. They took turns sleeping.
They were afraid. And they took turns sleeping and
when they were awake they would sit with a rifle staring
at the door. We found them there. Like the Three Fates
that passed their one eye between them.

(*Rest*)

Hero, when he was Hero, he met a Yankee. With two
blue coats. The Yankee had a friend and the friend had
a fever. He told me how he got the Yankee's coat. Such
a tall tall tale I didn't believe his story for a minute.
Anyhow. It was cold. Even in the summer. Old-Hero

put the blue coat underneath his grey coat. Kept his
own grey pants on though.

HOMER.

A Confederate from the waist down.

PENNY.

What?

THE RUNAWAY SLAVES.

He can read the signs.

HOMER.

What next, dog?

ODYSSEY DOG.

Hero distinguished himself. And he took a new name.

PENNY.

Hero took a new name?

ODYSSEY DOG.

In this one town, there was a slave gal. She sewed back
the buttons on Old-Hero's coat. I started to wonder
when it would end. I would dream of being back here.
Some fellows liked the War. Cannons be blazing! Towns
be burnt! Food was scarce. Hero shot a rabbit once.

PENNY.

And then he was shot!

HOMER.

Shot dead!

PENNY.

Go on and tell it! You hear me, just tell it!

ODYSSEY DOG.

Master got another horse. Called him Salute. One day
when Salute was running and Master was charging
and Old-Hero was running alongside Master and I
was running alongside Old-Hero and we were all one
fast moving cloud of black and grey and me and I was
thinking where the hell are we going and will we ever
get there? Then Old-Hero shouts, "Oh!"

PENNY.

And fell down dead.

ODYSSEY DOG.

Master had been hit.

HOMER.

Hero?

ODYSSEY DOG.

And Salute, not knowing any better just kept running.
And Old-Hero, Old-Hero—

PENNY.

Just say it! Just say it!

ODYSSEY DOG.

Master lay there bleeding. Master stanched the wound.
But. No use. The War continues on. Came back with
Master's body, just arrived today. Missus is beyond
consoling.

PENNY.

And my Hero: left dead on the field of battle for the
birds to eat out his eyes!

HOMER.

Hero's dead! God rest him!

ODYSSEY DOG.

Old-Hero?

No.

He'll be home directly.

PENNY.

Home directly?

ODYSSEY DOG.

I told it.

HOMER.

Home directly?

PENNY.

Home directly?

(**PENNY** *and* **HOMER** *embrace. Both begin to cry.*)

ODYSSEY DOG. *(Aside)*

Both are crying. I thought there'd be only one set of tears.

PENNY.

He's coming back? Don't lie to me.

ODYSSEY DOG.

He's coming back.

HOMER.

PENNY.

THE RUNAWAY SLAVES.

FIRST: We should go. Jet. Run.

SECOND: We should hide somewhere.

THIRD: From what they've said of Hero, how can we know we'll be safe?

HOMER.

It's not dark enough to travel yet. Still too much light in the sky.

PENNY.

I'll make him swear to keep your secret.

THE RUNAWAY SLAVES.

We thank you.

PENNY.

I'll run to meet him.

HOMER.

Stay here. Let him come in on his own.

Besides with the night coming and the road crawling

Crawling full of Patrollers,

It's safer to wait for him here.

PENNY.

You're right. I'll wait.

HOMER.

It's not dark enough. If it was, we could go.

PENNY.

You're still leaving.

HOMER.

And you'll stay.

PENNY.

I've got to stay now.

HOMER.

Alright.

PENNY.

But you'll be here when he comes. And you'll welcome
him with me. Then you'll go.

HOMER.

Then I'll go. Yeah.

HOMER.

PENNY.

PENNY.

I gotta go in and get things ready for him.

When he comes home things will be looking nice.

> *(Filled with excitement* **PENNY** *hurries inside to
> ready the house for the arrival.)*

HOMER.

Not dark enough.

Not dark enough.

Not dark enough to jet.

Not yet.

If I could pull the dark up. From wherever it is.

It's in the east. Where just this morning

Everything looked possible and pleasant

Now things look dark.

Or take some of my own dark

And smear it against the sky
To block the sun out
Just long enough to make it just safe enough to go
Not dark enough
Not dark enough yet
Not dark enough yet to jet.

THE RUNAWAY SLAVES.
FIRST: We could go now
THIRD: We could chance it
SECOND: We could throw caution to the wind
FIRST: We could run
THIRD: We could just walk on by
SECOND: We could go, Homer
FIRST: Help you ease your pain
SECOND: We'd be willing to risk it
THIRD: For you.

HOMER.
I want to be free
Not dead.
No, I'll wait.
It's just Hero I'll see.
I'll see them together and the sight will free me from
this place.
And I'll head out with you, all the surer, and we'll travel
all the faster.
Or maybe he won't even get here before nightfall
Maybe we'll already be on our way.
When him and Penny have their
Sweet reunion in the bed
Where she loved me but wouldn't
Love me.

ODYSSEY DOG.

Old-Hero Old-Hero Old-Hero Old-Hero.

> (**PENNY** *comes out of the house.*)

> (*She and* **ODYSSEY DOG** *run to greet the returning Soldier.*)

THE RUNAWAY SLAVES.

SECOND: The shape of a man
   On the horizon.

THIRD: And closer and closer and closer he comes

FIRST: Closer and closer and closer

FIRST, SECOND & THIRD: The Hero.

> (**PENNY** *re-enters followed by* **ULYSSES** *[formerly* **HERO***].*)

> (**ODYSSEY DOG** *follows behind.*)

PENNY.

Close your eyes. Hold my hand. Keep them closed! Now open them!

ULYSSES.

It looks the same.

PENNY.

It does. And so do you.

ULYSSES.

You're really here.

PENNY.

Yes.

(Rest)

Wrap your arms around me.

> (*He wraps her in his arms.*)

PENNY.

Look at me, I'm dancing you!

(She moves his arms, making him dance.)

(He lifts her up.)

ULYSSES.

And I'm flying you.

PENNY.

I'm a bird!

(They embrace. It's layered.)

PENNY.

ULYSSES.

ULYSSES.

Old folks dead?

PENNY.

Me and Homer's all that's left. And now you.

ULYSSES.

Homer.

HOMER.

Hero.

PENNY.

"Ulysses"!

HOMER.

Like the Union General!?

ULYSSES.

That's right!

HOMER.

You didn't!

ULYSSES.

I did.

PENNY.

The nerve.

ULYSSES.

You like Ulysses alright?

PENNY.

I do, but what'll Missus say?

ULYSSES.

I'll tell her when the time is right. If I choose to.

PENNY.

It'll take me some getting used to.

ULYSSES.

Take as long as you need.

(Rest)

Strangers, huh?

THE RUNAWAY SLAVES.

Yes.

ULYSSES.

Runaways?

HOMER.

You'll keep their secret safe.

ULYSSES.

Alright.

ULYSSES.

HOMER.

(Rest)

ULYSSES.

Every day, every day, I'm telling you, I prayed to just have the chance to come back here and show how I made good. And here I am, girl. Here I am.

PENNY.

I'll get a good supper on directly.

ULYSSES.

Course you will.

PENNY.

Look at you. Just look at you. My feelings are all over the place. I wish I was wearing something pretty.

ULYSSES.

You're pretty just like you are. Still just as pretty. Still just as strong.

(Rest)

Old folks really dead?

HOMER.

Dead or sold off.

ULYSSES.

The Old Man's dead too? Well. Colonel would mention from Missus' letters that someone had died or that someone had got sold but he wouldn't never tell me who it was by name.

PENNY.

I told you I would wait for you.

ULYSSES.

You did.

(Rest)

Penny.

PENNY.

Hero.

(Rest)

"Ulysses."

I feel like you'll always be "Hero" to me.

ULYSSES.

Ulysses suits me and I chose it for myself. Any of you ever done that? Choose your own name? No, right? It's really something. Take all the time you need getting used to it.

HOMER.

Might take a lifetime.

ULYSSES.

Hopefully less than that.

HOMER.

Welcome home.

ULYSSES.

I thank you.

> (**ULYSSES** *kneels on the ground. He gets up. He kneels again.*)

ULYSSES.

This is what I seen them do. When they get home. I'm just following but it feels right.

> (*He kisses the ground.*)

> (*Then he sees* **HOMER***'s writing.*)

> (**HOMER** *erases the letters with his foot.*)

ULYSSES.
HOMER.

ULYSSES.

"Penny"?

HOMER.

I was just—

PENNY.

Look at you. Just look at you.

ULYSSES.

Just look at you.

> (*Rest*)

Penny.

PENNY.

That's right.

ULYSSES.

And Oddsee came back to me alright. And he sure was my luck cause here I am.

ODYSSEY DOG.

Here I am. Here I am.

ULYSSES.

And he ran ahead like I told him. To tell you I was on my way.

PENNY.

Yes.

ULYSSES.

They're hanging black crepe at the Master's house. They'll lay him in the ground tomorrow.

HOMER.

I suppose you'll help dig his grave.

ULYSSES.

I will. We'll dig it together.

HOMER.

Huh.

(Rest)

You're back. That's really something.

ULYSSES.

It's the War that's really Something, I'm telling you.

THE RUNAWAY SLAVES.

FIRST: We'll be gone by nightfall.

SECOND: In case you're wondering.

THIRD: And we're good honest people.

FIRST: Just like you.

ULYSSES.

We can't help you but so much.

THE RUNAWAY SLAVES.

SECOND: Not telling that we were ever here.

THIRD: And helping us hide until nightfall, that's kindness enough.

FIRST: And we, in turn, will keep your kindness secret.

ULYSSES.

We thank you.

(Rest)

I got stories. But I'll save them. So many stories. Most of them unspeakable but I suppose in time I'll find a way to tell. Like what I said to a Yankee when I met him face to face. And other things. I'll be an old man on this porch surrounded by his children telling war stories. I'll tell everything to the children.

PENNY.

The children.

ULYSSES.

That'll be something, won't it?

(Rest)

How you been Homer?

HOMER.

I've been alright.

ULYSSES.

Working hard or hardly working?

HOMER.

Working hard.

ULYSSES.

And still here, huh?

HOMER.

Still here, yeah.

ULYSSES.

I brought home presents.

HOMER.

I'm gonna be heading out with them. Just so you know. We'd go right this minute but—

ULYSSES.

You leaving with them?

You be safe, hear?

And I'll keep your secret.

HOMER.

That's your Word?

ULYSSES.

That's my Word.

HOMER.

Alright.

ULYSSES.

In the meantime gather round. I brought you something. I brought you something too, Penny. Something for everybody. Come on, gather round.

(They gather around **ULYSSES.***)*

(He's like a king graciously holding forth.)

HOMER.

Oddsee says it's a Yankee coat you wore underneath your Rebel one.

ULYSSES.

You told them that, Oddsee?

ODYSSEY DOG.

I did. I did.

ULYSSES.

Yeah, it's true. Take a look.

(He removes his Confederate Army coat, revealing the Union Army coat underneath.)

ULYSSES.

It kept me good and warm, and, you know, it was a sort of Truth for me.

(Rest)

Did Oddsee tell you how I freed a man?

HOMER.

You freed a man?

ULYSSES.

I did.

ODYSSEY DOG.

Such a tall tall tale.

ULYSSES.

I really did.

(Rest)

But there'll be plenty of time to talk more about that. Plenty of time for more stories.

(Rest)

Homer, this here's for you.

> *(From his satchel, he pulls out a foot, more like a shoe last, made of white alabaster.)*

HOMER.

A foot.

THE RUNAWAY SLAVES.

FIRST: Not dark enough

THIRD: Not yet

SECOND: Not dark enough to jet.

HOMER.

A foot. I thank you.

ULYSSES.

They use it to model shoes on. The shop had burned to the ground. I seen it laying in the ash. Let it take the place of the one you lost.

HOMER.

I didn't lose it. Wasn't like I woke up one morning and couldn't remember where I put it.

ULYSSES.

Well, you know.

(Rest)

It's made of alabaster. It's worth a lot.

HOMER.

I thank you.

ULYSSES.

HOMER.

(Rest)

ULYSSES.

And for Penny:

> *(From his satchel, he takes out a silver-tipped gardening spade.)*

PENNY.

A spade.

ULYSSES.

Silver-tipped.

PENNY.

Silver! It's lovely.

ULYSSES.

And you're only allowed to use it for your garden. And the garden's gonna have rules: I don't want you just planting vegetables with it. I want you to put some flowers in the ground too. Lots of flowers.

PENNY.

I knew you'd come home.

ULYSSES.

And here I am. I brought presents for everybody if they'd been here— A string of brass buttons! A shiny new spoon! The best present I brought is writ down right here.

> *(**ULYSSES** takes a piece of paper from his breast coat pocket.)*

> *(He looks at it. **HOMER** and **PENNY** look on.)*

THE RUNAWAY SLAVES.

FIRST: We can read.

SECOND: Show us.

THIRD: Or just tell us what it says.

ULYSSES.

I'll read it to you.

>   *(But instead of reading it aloud he holds the paper close.)*

>   *(He savors his power in the moment and their expectant looks, then decides to discuss another subject instead.)*

ULYSSES.

THE RUNAWAY SLAVES.

HOMER.

PENNY.

ULYSSES.

>   *(Rest)*

ULYSSES.

But first. Well, I brought something for Homer, and I brought something for you too, Penny. This here paper says something for all of us, but first, well, I brought something home for me too. Sit down, Penny.

PENNY.

Your presents gonna sweep me off my feet I wanna get swept.

ULYSSES.

Sit down.

PENNY.

Alright.

>   *(**PENNY** sits down. **ULYSSES** takes a small photograph from his pocket. He looks at it before showing it to **PENNY**.)*

ULYSSES.

Her name's Alberta. The Missus will bring her over here in a couple of days.

PENNY.

She's pretty. Who is she?

ULYSSES.

Alberta. She's a nice gal. Real nice.

PENNY.

Who is she aside from nice?

ULYSSES.

She's my new wife.

PENNY.

New—

HOMER.

New wife?

PENNY.

I'm— But I'm—

ULYSSES.

You and me, Penny, we don't have no kids. Can't, right? You're still just as pretty still just as strong, but I was thinking it would be good to have children. I was thinking— I know you'll understand. You're good and true like that. Alberta, she'll help you around here. When planting time comes she'll do her part and work right along beside you. And with Homer heading out, we'll need an extra hand. She'll be a help to both of us.

PENNY.

But I'm—me.

ULYSSES.

And I'm giving you the better part of the deal, Penny. You can't say that I'm not.

PENNY.

Hero. I mean—

ULYSSES.

I'm giving you the advantage in this. You're getting the upper hand. I haven't told her about you. Not yet. And I won't. Not until she gets here. You're hearing the news first. You got the upper hand on it. So you can prepare yourself. And by the time she gets here, Lord, you'll have it all figured out. What her chores are and and and, and all the rest.

HOMER.

Where will she sleep?

ULYSSES.

That's not for you to ask.

PENNY.

Where will she sleep?

ULYSSES.

She'll sleep with me.

(Rest)

I went to the War and I came back here, I had to, but I didn't have to, but I did, and not knowing who or what I'd find waiting for me and so I did the best I could and just came home with presents. I figured there's no sense in making it all the way through and then come home to watch myself die off. That's how I figured it, anyways.

PENNY.

That's how you figured it.

ULYSSES.

Yes.

PENNY.

You changed. You changed everything. Everything about you went down the road. Where'd you go? Away. Now you're back. But you're not back, are you?

ULYSSES.

I'm standing right here.

PENNY.

I'm right here too! And I'm still me. And I'm still living. And I'm still here.

ULYSSES.

Put a good face on it, girl. Please.

PENNY.

The face I got isn't good enough, I guess. So I'll work on it. Change it. Make it into something better. How about a smile? All the days I waited for you. Smile. The months I waited for you. Smile. All that time. And every time we heard of someone dead I prayed it wasn't you. Smile. I worked hard while you was gone. I minded the Missus like you told me to. Like you told me to. Smile. Smile. Smile. I hate you.

> *(**PENNY** cries. **HOMER** comforts her.)*

> *(**ULYSSES** watches **HOMER** and **PENNY**.)*

> *(He doesn't like what he's seeing.)*

HOMER.

We could go. Now.

PENNY.

Not me. No. And crying isn't gonna help. Why I thought I deserved something special, I'll never know. I'll go inside and make the house ready. For you and for your new bride. You can count on me, Old-Hero, to do at least that.

> *(She dutifully goes into the house.)*

THE RUNAWAY SLAVES.

FIRST: You haven't heard the old stories
    But I have.

SECOND: You don't know the old stories
    But I do.

THIRD: Old stories, they guide us
    Each its own North Star
    You don't know them
    And how could you?

SECOND: They happened so far back
FIRST: Years ago

THIRD: Years and years ago

SECOND: Years and years and years ago

THIRD: What could they have to do with you?

SECOND: I'm scared of what will happen next.

> The old story guides me to a dangerous place
> A place I head to by homing habit.
> Not like the journey I'm on now, right?

THIRD: The place I'm going now is Freedom

SECOND: But where is Freedom, really?

> Will the air smell sweet?
> Will the streets be paved with gold?
> Will all in Freedomville welcome me with open arms?
> Will there be food?
> Will there be a bed to lay my Freedom Head?

FIRST: Freedom will swell me, maybe

> Maybe it will burst my brains to madness
> Maybe it will flood my heart to death
> Will I say, at the end of the day,
> "God, I wish I'd stayed home?"

SECOND: I'm afraid of what will happen next.

THIRD: Inside, Penny makes up the marriage bed

> And in doing so she takes her place in a long line of
> the Wronged.
> Come out of the house, true wife, true love,

SECOND: Come with us

FIRST: Come with us

THIRD: Come break the chain.

> *(Rest)*

FIRST: I wish it was dark enough

THIRD: I wish it was dark enough

SECOND: Dark enough to jet.

FIRST, SECOND & THIRD: Not yet

> Not yet
> Not yet
> Not yet.

HOMER.

It will be soon.

FIRST RUNAWAY.

Homer help us

Come here and help us plan the way.

Let's ready ourselves together.

HOMER.

I'm figuring the best way for us. There's a kind of trick to it. We gotta be looking for the signs all the time and in everything. And if one way fails we gotta find another one. That'll be the Way we go. I'll show you how we'll do it.

THE RUNAWAY SLAVES.

We thank you.

> (**HOMER** *joins* **THE RUNAWAY SLAVES.** *They speak apart, making plans.*)

> (**ULYSSES,** *standing apart, speaks with* **ODYSSEY DOG.**)

ULYSSES.

He bothers me.

(Rest)

You saw him and her? Homer and Penny hugging together?

ODYSSEY DOG.

I didn't see. I didn't see.

ULYSSES.

Yes you did. You're not blind.

ODYSSEY DOG.

Penny cried. She's sad. Homer, he held her. They're friends. That's all.

ULYSSES.

She wasn't faithful to me.

ODYSSEY DOG.

Who can know? A hug is just a hug.

ULYSSES.

It tells me more than that. I know.

ODYSSEY DOG.

You can't be sure. And besides. You weren't faithful either.

(**ULYSSES** *kicks his dog.*)

ULYSSES.

Remember your place, dog.

ODYSSEY DOG.

ULYSSES.

ODYSSEY DOG.

Faithful, huh. You went to the War and you coulda been anywhere. I looked for you. I smelled you out. The grass was green and soft in some places and in other places it was brown and crinkly. And I followed you and I found you. That's faithful.

(Rest)

For me, faithful is easy. It's easy for a dog to be faithful. Don't ask me why but it's true. Faithful for a dog comes natural. Like to a man such as you comes walking upright. Faithful is in a dog's bones. We're all born to do it. Can't be broke. But for a man or a woman person, faithful comes extra. Like speech comes extra for me. It's not a given. And what is faithful, anyway, when there's a war on? There's a home-way and a war-way. They're different. Be kind, Old-Hero. Be kind. You're home.

ULYSSES.

He bothers me. Cause of Penny? Maybe. Or maybe that's just the start of it.

ODYSSEY DOG.

Leave it. Leave it.

ULYSSES.

Homer?

> (**HOMER** *steps away from* **THE RUNAWAY SLAVES** *to speak with* **ULYSSES.**)

HOMER.

We'll be gone soon, if you're wondering.

ULYSSES.

Did you sleep with my wife?

HOMER.

Your picture wife?

ULYSSES.

Penny, I'm talking about.

HOMER.

It's Penny who should be in that picture. Not that other gal.

ULYSSES.

Did you love my Penny yes or no?

HOMER.

She needed someone. She chose me. She needs someone now, but you've moved on. How you gonna bear that? How she's gonna bear that, I don't know. But it's not my place to know. My place is somewhere better. And she's staying here with you cause she's true like that, all right?

ULYSSES.

Yeah. Go on then.

HOMER.

Tell me something.

ULYSSES.

What.

HOMER.

Did he ever get around to freeing you?

ULYSSES.

No. He didn't.

HOMER.

ULYSSES.

ULYSSES.

He didn't give me my freedom.

(Rest)

Not even with his dying breath.

In spite of all his promises.

And what beautiful promises they were.

With every day they grew fuller and riper.

I'd imagine sitting at a head of a fine table and eating
my fill

That's how real they were. I could taste them.

And when I'd wake up my mouth was only full of my
own teeth

And tongue and spit. And my stomach growled.

And he'd feed it. With promises. And I would feast on
them.

I don't take after him in looks but I did take after him.

I did. I did. Following in his every footstep.

My stride got to be the same as his.

And sometimes I'd hear myself laughing and think,
that's the Colonel,

No that's me.

Can you imagine? Can you see it?

Funny.

I should have killed him.

I had the chance more than once but didn't.

And when he finally died

I thought for a minute I'd follow him into the grave

That's how close we were.

You,

You make me think of how I wronged you.

I see you and I see my faults.

Funny.

Just like with me and Master:

I'd always, just by being myself, I'd always be somehow reminding him

Of his Faults against me.

And so, to make it all right, to make it bearable, so I could find a way to breathe

I went and I cut out my soul.

I cut my soul out of myself.

And I gave it up to him.

Or I lost it.

You're lucky. You're going to a better place.

HOMER.

Freedom's better than this.

ULYSSES.

How you know for sure? How you know?

HOMER.

I just know, that's all. In my heart. I know.

ULYSSES.

It's dark enough, Homer. You better get going. Go on to that better place and go there quick.

>   (**ULYSSES** *takes out his knife. He lunges at* **HOMER,** *intent on killing him. They struggle.*)

HOMER.

No!

THE RUNAWAY SLAVES.

No! No!

ODYSSEY DOG.

No!

>   (**PENNY** *comes out of the house.*)

PENNY.

No!!!

PENNY.
ULYSSES.

(Rest)

PENNY.
No.

PENNY.
ULYSSES.
HOMER.
PENNY.

(Rest)

ULYSSES.
PENNY.

(**ULYSSES** *withdraws his knife.*)

PENNY.
All that time of waiting and wishing and praying that
   you were alive
And I was in our house just now
Praying you was dead.
And all those times I would lay with you, Homer,
Praying you was him.
God must not of heard me right.
My prayers got confused.
My prayers got confused.

THE RUNAWAY SLAVES.
FIRST: Now the sun is down
   The day has pulled a blanket over its own head

THIRD: Wish us good luck

FIRST: Wish us good fortune

SECOND: Wish us safety

FIRST: Wish us food and water along the way

THIRD: Wish us Freedom

SECOND: Wish us open arms when we arrive

FIRST: Wish us work. Wish us luck

THIRD: Wish us a way to get our families back

SECOND: Wish us at least that. Wish us at least that.

HOMER.

We're heading out. We'll go.

PENNY.

Yes. We'll go.

ULYSSES.

You'll stay, Penny. Please. I don't want you going.

> (**ULYSSES** *takes* **PENNY**'s *hand but* **PENNY** *pulls away.*)

> (*She tears a piece from her dress, handing it to* **ULYSSES**.)

PENNY.

I'm leaving. I'm gone. Let's go.

> (**PENNY** *leaves with* **HOMER** *and* **THE RUNAWAY SLAVES**.)

> (**ULYSSES** *and* **ODYSSEY DOG** *are alone.*)

ODYSSEY DOG.

There are worse things. I dunno what but there are worse things.

ULYSSES.

ULYSSES.

ULYSSES.

>   (**ULYSSES** *takes that paper out, looks it over.*)

ULYSSES.

>   This paper. I never got to read it to them.

>   The Proclamation. I copied it down.

>   *(Rest)*

>   It says we're free.

ODYSSEY DOG.

>   The Runaways, they still got to run.

ULYSSES.

>   Still and all.

>   *(Rest)*

>   These are my hands now.

>   *(Rest)*

>   I'll bury the Boss-Master.

ODYSSEY DOG.

>   I'll help.

>   (**ULYSSES** *looks toward Boss-Master's house, ready to undertake his new life.*)

>   (**ODYSSEY DOG** *holds the spade.*)

End of Play

DARK IS THE NIGHT

Suzan-Lori Parks
transcribed by Steven Bargonetti

DARK IS THE NIGHT

LONG IS THE DAY -

DARK IS THE NIGHT - LONG IS THE DAY -

- GOT TIME FOR WORK - NO TIME TO PRAY -

HE'S LEAVING

Suzan-Lori Parks
transcribed by Steven Bargonetti

Andante (Doubletime country blues, rockabilly feel) ♩ = 93

HE'S LEAVING

Instrumental Break

FAR THER AND FAR - THER HE'LL BE

GO - ING... FAR-THER AND FAR-THER DOWN THE WAY

FAR-THER AND FAR-THER___ GONE-GONE GONE ON DOWN THE WAY-

- - LORD GIVE HIM GOOD COM-PAN-Y NOW

CAUSE HE WON'T BE HOME TO DAY___

PASSING THE TIME

The Colonel's Song
(repeat for each verse)

Suzan-Lori Parks

Like a Cowboy Song

The Colonel

(cowboy swing -starts freely)

I'VE SAT ON_____ A MOUN-TAIN_ I'VE SAT ON_____ A HILL I LOVE GOD_____ AND COUN-TRY_____ I PAY ALL_ MY BILLS - - I'M A PRET-TY_____ GOOD HUS - BAND, THOUGH DON'T ASK_ MY WIFE IF SHE CAT - CHES ME HERE, I'LL PAY WITH MY LIFE.

THIS BRIGHT WILDERNESS

Suzan-Lori Parks

transcribed by Steven Bargonetti

Andante (Folk feel) ♩ = 90

THIS BRIGHT WILDERNESS

DARK - EST OF THE DARK - EST NIGHT THERE IS STILL A DAY THAT
THICK IS THIN AND THE PLEN - TY ENDS IT WILL BE WHAT IT HAS

COMES ALL RIGHT. GOD IS IN HIS HEA - VEN UP A - BOVE
AL - WAYS BEEN

UP A - BOVE WHILE WE TOIL BRAVE - LY DOWN BE - LOW

1st ending

2nd ending

2. WHEN THE LOW GOD IS IN HIS HEA - VEN UP A - BOVE-

UP A - BOVE WHILE WE TOIL BRAVE - LY DOWN BE - LOW .

Gtr.

MISPLACED MYSELF
Odyssey Dog's Theme

Suzan-Lori Parks
transcribed by Steven Bargonetti

Vivace (Texas shuffle feel) ♩ = 160

MISPLACED MYSELF

SEAR-CHING ON THE RI - VERS THEY BE QUES-TION - ING THE BEES I'M

LOO - ONG GONE I AIN'T SIT - TING ON YOUR SHELF

I HAVE MI - PLACED MY - SELF - - -

- I HAVE MIS - PLACED MY - SELF

HERO'S THEME

Suzan-Lori Parks
transcribed by Steven Bargonetti

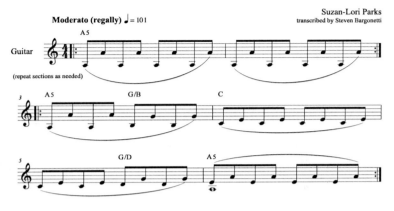

PENNY'S THEME

Suzan-Lori Parks
transcribed by Steven Bargonetti

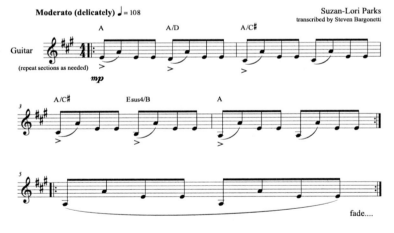

LEAVE ALL THIS BEHIND
Runaway's Theme

Suzan-Lori Parks
transcribed by Steven Bargonetti

KISS

Suzan-Lori Parks
transcribed by Steven Bargonetti

OLD STORIES

Suzan-Lori Parks
transcribed by Steven Bargonetti

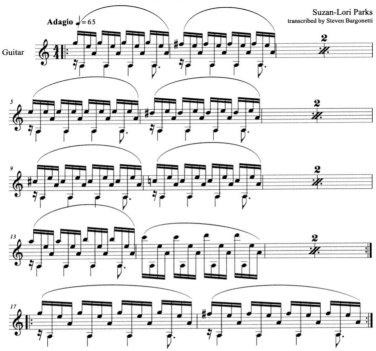

keep repeating, rit. and fade........

PASSING INTO WILDERNESS

Suzan-Lori Parks
transcribed by Steven Bargonetti

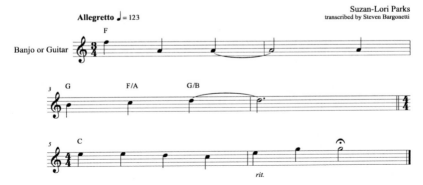

BRONZE STAR THEME

HOMER'S THEME